MONDEGREENS

Mondegreen *n.* a word or phrase that is misinterpreted as another word or phrase, usually with an amusing result.

Collins English Dictionary, 2005

MONDEGREENS

A Book of Mishearings

J. A. WINES

MICHAEL O'MARA BOOKS LIMITED

First published in Great Britain in 2007 by
Michael O'Mara Books Limited
9 Lion Yard, Tremadoc Road
London SW4 7NQ

A CIP catalogue record for this book is available
from the British Library

Papers used by Michael O'Mara Books Limited are
natural, recyclable products made from wood grown
in sustainable forests. The manufacturing processes
conform to the environmental regulations of the
country of origin.

ISBN 978-1-84317-235-2

3 5 7 9 10 8 6 4 2

www.mombooks.com

Designed and typeset by Martin Bristow

Printed and bound in Great Britain
by Clays Ltd, St Ives plc

Contents

CONTENTS

Author Acknowledgements

——

THE AUTHOR would like to thank the many people who kindly proffered numerous mondegreens and mishearings for this book (too many of you to name here individually), and to apologize to those whose conversations have been listened in to for many months. You are off the hook for now.

Special thanks to Toby and Helen for your help and encouragement in putting together this book.

Lady Mondegreen:
An Introduction

━━━━

THE WORD 'mondegreen' was coined by an American
writer, Sylvia Wright. When she was a child her mother
had read aloud to her from Thomas Percy's *Reliques of
Ancient English Poetry* (1765), which included the Scottish
ballad 'The Bonny Earl of Murray'. Wright was particularly fond of this ballad, which she thought included the
following stanza:

> 'Ye Highlands and ye Lowlands,
> Oh, where hae you been?
> They hae slain the Earl Amurray [*sic*],
> And Lady Mondegreen.'

In Wright's imagination, Lady Mondegreen was a tragic
heroine – murdered alongside her husband by the Gordon
henchmen of the Earl of Huntly in the late 1500s.
Unsurprisingly, Wright was distressed to discover in later
life that Lady Mondegreen had in fact never existed; rather
she was the creation of Wright's mishearing of the words
'They hae slain the Earl of Murray, / And laid him on the
green.'

Wright was not ready to give up on her heroine lightly.
In November 1954 she penned an article, 'The Death of
Lady Mondegreen', for *Harper's Magazine*, which struck a
chord with her readers, many of whom had also fallen

victim to an aural 'trick'. Thus the mondegreen was given life.

Technically, a mondegreen is the mishearing of a phrase in such a way that it is understood to have an alternative meaning. This often occurs because the English language is rich in homophones – words which may not be the same in origin, spelling or meaning, but which sound the same.

As an example, when I was describing the origin of the word 'mondegreen' to a friend, she confused my words 'yes, she was all in Wright's mind', with the expression 'to be in one's right mind', which of course wasn't the way I'd meant it. A slight mishearing, and her choice of the most likely match for what I'd said, had led us away from the original meaning.

Many mondegreens occur when listeners are distracted. Perhaps my friend was only listening with half an ear to what I was saying, her busy mind temporarily elsewhere. On the other hand, I could have chosen my words more carefully. Many mondegreens involve food, probably because the listener was hungry at the time and the subject of food was at the forefront of their mind. Likewise, innocent lyrics often acquire a sexual connotation.

On other occasions mondegreens occur due to ignorance of what is being said. Children, for example, will match the most logical explanation to the words they hear, often mistakenly. Surprisingly, many adults are not immune to this type of mishearing, even when they really should know better. Accents and dialects also create confusion, and naturally it doesn't help when one is hard of hearing.

In Sylvia Wright's case, the loss of Lady Mondegreen was a disappointment, while, for others, mishearings have led to embarrassment, confusion, a trip up the garden path, or have even been a matter of life or death. Nevertheless, we shouldn't forget that mondegreens can be hugely entertaining, as well as being great examples of wordplay.

Finally, many people labour under the misconception that mondegreens can only derive from the mishearing of song lyrics. This is not the case, although thousands of them are created this way, and some of the best of these are to be found in these pages – alongside many famous, infamous and everyday examples of conversations that went awry.

'He that hath ears to hear, let him hear.'

Matthew 11:15, THE BIBLE

Mondegreens
in their Infancy

The 'awful' job of looking after children

A *Times* reader wrote to the newspaper in 2001 to tell how, some years before, his wife had been the victim of a mishearing. She had telephoned her local paper to place an advertisement for help with three small children, and she had specifically asked for the advert to include the phrase, 'requires help for three or four hours a week'. However, when she purchased a copy of the paper, she was surprised to read that she required 'help for three awful hours a week'. Interestingly, though, she had plenty of enquiries about the position.

ജന

Hold tight to the meaning

A harassed mother was observed trying to keep her patience while her three young children resisted her efforts to get them into the car. One of the children ran off down the pavement and took a nasty tumble.

'Oops, that one's gone flying!' remarked a well-intentioned passer-by.

To which the mother retorted, 'I *know* they're not bloody complying.'

Ꙩ

Mother love and bear hugs

In the 1890s, a writer in the *Church Times* dubbed a popular Anglican hymn – 'Hark, My Soul, It Is the Lord' by William Cowper – the 'She-bear hymn'. The third verse begins: 'Can a woman's tender care cease towards the child she bear?'

In a letter to *The Independent*, a reader described the same mondegreen from her schooldays, which in her vivid imagination had conjured up bizarre visions of a bear cub in a frilly dress being looked after by its human mother.

> 'The cave-man may have been no better than the cave-bear; but the child she-bear, so famous in hymnology, is not trained with any such bias for spinsterhood.'
>
> G. K. CHESTERTON, *The Everlasting Man*

However, the most often quoted mondegreen is probably 'Gladly the cross-eyed bear', a mishearing of the line 'Kept by Thy tender care, gladly the cross I'll bear' from the hymn 'Keep Thou My Way' by Fanny Crosby. Ed McBain used the mondegreen as the title of a novel (*Gladly the Cross-Eyed Bear*, 1996), and the cross-eyed bear makes a brief appearance ('behind the stairs') in the song 'Hide Away Folk Family' by the band They Might Be Giants.

What Mother didn't say

'When I was little, my mother would always tell me that my room "looked like a bomb's hit it". It was only in my mid-teens that I realized that "Abombsitit" wasn't an actual place.'

☆

'My mother used to tell me not to stand there like "two orvils waiting for the gravy". I understood that this meant I should jump, but I never knew what an "orvil" was. I had a mental picture of a gryphon or a gargoyle. Maybe because "orvil" sounds a bit like "evil", or because I was being ticked off and the experience was unpleasant. However, when I was small there was also a children's television programme that starred a green chick called Orville, so I had that in mind too. When I was a teenager, it finally occurred to me to query the physical representation of an "orvil". My mother stared at me blankly and suggested that I ask my grandmother. "You daft idiot," said Nan, laughing. "She means two of eels waiting for the gravy, Lord love a duck!" I have to say that discovering that "orvils" were eels was disappointing. I never did ask her to explain the duck reference.'

'When I took my young children to see my mother recently, she told me she had moved her china ornaments (which they can't resist touching) out of harm's way. My mother drops her aitches, and funnily enough, it only hit me at that moment that I'd always thought she was saying, "out of arm's sway". This seems just as good to me.'

'We learn something every day, and lots of times it's that what we learned the day before was wrong.'

BILL VAUGHAN

Children's Songs
and Nursery Rhymes

────

Some that went astray

────

**'Mary had a little lamb
Its fleece was white as snow'**

'Mary had a little lamb
Its *fleas* were white as snow'

'Mary had a little lamb
Its fleece was *right as new*'

**'Do you know the muffin man
Who lives on Drury Lane?'**

'Do you know the muffin man
Who lives *under Elaine*?'

'Here we go round the mulberry bush'

'Here we go round the *mouldy* bush'

'It's raining, it's pouring . . .'

'It's raining, it's *boring* . . .'

'The clock struck one, the mouse ran down'

'The clock struck one, the mouse *was dead*'

'Heads, shoulders, knees and toes, knees and toes'

'Head, shoulders, *sneeze* and toes, *sneeze* and toes'

'And one for the little boy, who lives down the lane'

'And one for the little boy, *because he is lame*'

'And one for the little boy, who lives down the *drain*'

**'There was a farmer, had a dog
And Bingo was his name-o'**

'There was a farmer, had a dog
And Bingo was his *game-o*'

'The farmer's in the dell'

'The farmer's in, *all yell*'

'The farmer wants a wife'

'The farmer *chews his* wife'

'The farmer *shoots the* wife'

**'Little Miss Muffet,
Sat on a tuffet,
Eating her curds and whey'**

'Little Miss Muffet,
Sat on a tuffet,
Eating her *curtains away*'

'Row, row, row your boat, gently down the stream'

'Row, row, row your boat, gently down the *street*'

☆

**'Sonnez les matines, sonnez les matines,
Ding, dang, dong' (from 'Frère Jacques')**

'Funny lemon tea please, funny lemon tea please,
Ding, dang, dong'

☆

**'Lavender's blue, dilly dilly,
Lavender's green'**

'*Laugh and turn blue*, dilly dilly,
Laugh and turn green'

[18]

What larks?

'My six-year-old daughter Honor started French classes last year and I was amused to hear her singing the words to "Sur Le Pont d'Avignon". Her version goes:

Sur le pont d'Avignon
Honor dances, Honor dances
(L'on y danse, l'on y danse)

Sur le pont d'Avignon
Honnie dances too around
(L'on y danse tous en rond)

'Funnily enough, it was not long before Jonty, my five-year-old, also found himself a French song. He is now frequently heard belting out "Alouette, Jonty alouette (*gentille alouette*) / Alouette Jonty oo arr HEY!" (*Je te plumerai*).'

In the Classroom

Ducking the meaning . . .

'No ducks or hazards' is a common though ludicrous mishearing of '*no dark sarcasm* in the classroom' from Pink Floyd's 'Another Brick in the Wall'.

> TEACHER: 'Who can use the word "antennae" in a sentence?'
> PUPIL: 'There antennae good sentences I can think of.'

Rote on

Never having found learning 'by heart' particularly easy, a lady of a certain age admitted that for all of her young school life, she understood that she must memorize certain poems and passages from literature 'by hard'.

Another former pupil misheard the expression 'to do things by half'. He too heard 'by hard'. He left school understanding that he should not approach tasks that were too difficult for him. It wasn't until later in life that he understood he had only been putting in half the understanding, as well as half the effort.

I was rescued at last by a gracious lady – the sixteen-year-old junior teacher – who boxed a few ears and dried my face and led me off to The Infants. I spent that first day picking holes in paper, then went home in a smouldering temper.

'What's the matter, Loll? Didn't he like it at school, then?'

'They never gave me the present!'

'Present? What present?'

'They said they'd give me a present.'

'Well, now, I'm sure they didn't.'

'They did! They said: "You're Laurie Lee, ain't you? Well, just you sit there for the present." I sat there all day but I never got it. I ain't going back there again!'

Extract from *Cider with Rosie* by LAURIE LEE
(London, 1959, Hogarth Press)

One chap recalls a revelation he had in later life: 'When I was at school, my English teacher once said we should learn a poem "by rote". I thought she said we should learn a poem "I wrote". The next day I stood up and voiced my feeble effort. "Excellent, Roy," said the teacher. Years later, I was looking up something in the dictionary when I came across the word "rote" and the scales fell from my eyes!'

☆

Now in his adult years, a certain gentleman has never got over the embarrassment of – having been asked to learn a passage 'by rote' – asking his teacher who 'Rote' was.

CB8O

As easy as A, B, C

Children are often encouraged to sing the alphabet. Many, however, get stuck on the letters 'L, M, N, O, P', as these offerings show:

'Elly, belly, bee'

'Yellow, mellow, pee'

'I'm a little bee'

'Elementary'

'Letter "B", letter "B", letter "B", letter "B"'

A mishearing of The Beatles' song 'Let It Be'
(also misheard as 'Ecstasy')

When singing the well-known 'ABC Song' to the tune of 'Twinkle, Twinkle, Little Star', many kids have mistakenly reached the conclusion that 'L–M–N–O–P', which is sung twice as fast as the other letters in the alphabet, is a word in its own right, spelled 'elemenopee'.

Things they didn't hear from us

'This is a picture of an octopus. It has eight testicles.'

(KELLY, age six)

☆

'If you are surrounded by sea you are an island. If you don't have sea all round you, you are incontinent.'

(WAYNE, age seven)

☆

'A dolphin breathes through an arsehole on the top of its head.'

(BILLY, age eight)

☆

Child telling her mother why her swimming lesson has been cancelled:

'Mummy, it's because the pool is constipated.'

School talk

MOTHER: 'My son tells me this year's charity walk is to the pool. Is that the school pool?'

TEACHER: 'Actually, it's to Nepal. We want to raise money for our sister school there.'

MOTHER, embarrassed: 'I see. I thought it wouldn't have been much of a walk.'

FIRST CHILD: 'Mummy, my friend was sick today. Mrs Pallett says there's a bug going round the school.'

SECOND CHILD: 'Yes, I think it's a snail.'

'When we were little,' the Mock Turtle went on at last, more calmly, though still sobbing a little now and then, 'we went to school in the sea. The master was an old Turtle – we used to call him Tortoise –'

'Why did you call him Tortoise, if he wasn't one?' Alice asked.

'We called him Tortoise because he taught us,' said the Mock Turtle angrily: 'really you are very dull!'

Extract from *Alice in Wonderland*
by LEWIS CARROLL

Monstrous headmasters

In his poem 'Blue Umbrellas' D. J. Enright (1920–2002), somewhat regretfully, informs his three-year-old daughter, who has just been introduced to the mysteries of school, that when referring to the man in charge, 'Head Monster is not the gentleman's accepted title.'

> *'I'd like to teach the world to sing in perfect harm and me'*
>
> A mishearing of the song 'I'd Like to Teach the World to Sing (in Perfect Harmony)', made famous by The New Seekers

Did I Hear That Right?

> 'Words, as is well known, are the great foes of reality.'
>
> JOSEPH CONRAD

SOMETIMES one hears a sentence where it is difficult to tell where one word ends and the next begins. Obviously such occasions are ripe for mishearings, as the following examples show:

She made a mistake, which led to his death.
She made him a steak, which led to his death.

The good can decay many ways.
The good candy came anyways.

I need to get her address.
I need to get her a dress.

The stuff he knows can lead to problems.
The stuffy nose can lead to problems.

[26]

Some others I've seen.
Some mothers I've seen.

I have a notion how they got there.
I have an ocean how they got there.

Mr Brown is out standing in his field.
Mr Brown is outstanding in his field.

The women also.
The women all sew.

'You're the devil in disguise'
'You're the devil in the skies'
(A mishearing from Madonna's 'Beautiful Stranger')

'Maybe you should take a leave'

Mondegreen that originated after the
anti-inflammatory drug naproxen sodium
became available over the counter as Aleve

Computer glitch

It's hard to recognize speech.
It's hard to wreck a nice beach.

The above example allegedly originated from one of the earliest computer speech-recognition programs. Supposedly, it was presented at a demo, and the words were printed on a T-shirt given to Apple engineers who worked on the company's early speech-recognition software. The naked version is:

This new display can recognize speech.
This nudist play can wreck a nice beach.

Hearing you loud and clear . . .

☆ The ultimate in convenience can be the ultimate inconvenience.

☆ To all intents and purposes it's for all intensive purposes.

☆ Diarrhoea may lead to a dire rear.

☆ I scream for ice cream.

☆ Since time immemorial we've spent time in memorial.

Brought to Book

'Paperback Writer' by The Beatles has not only been mis-heard as 'Paperback Biter', but also as 'Piggyback Rider' . . .

Sign language

At a book signing in 1964, author Monica Dickens was handed a book by a woman whom she thought had said, 'Emma Chisit'. Monica signed the book 'To Emma Chisit', before realizing that what the woman had actually said was 'How much is it?'

Grin and bear it . . .

'When I was at school we were studying Shakespeare's *Julius Caesar* for our English O level. It was a long, boring afternoon as we read round the class and various pupils stuttered over the language. I was doodling on the book when my English teacher suddenly asked me to explain the text: "Did from the flames of Troy upon his shoulder / The old Anchises bear, so from the waves of Tiber." Of course, had I been paying attention, I wouldn't have mentioned anything remotely associated with grizzly bears . . .'

Smash and grab

Someone else had a problem with Shakespeare's Roman masterpiece: 'Until I got hold of a copy of the play and read the title, I'd never thought of "Caesar" as a name,' she admitted. 'I thought the words were "Julius, seize her . . ."'

'Who sober sat around with dismal stories'

A mishearing of the line 'Who so beset him round with dismal stories', from John Bunyan's hymn 'He Who Would Valiant Be'

Mistitled

Donkey Hote – DON JUAN (*Don Quixote*)

The Oranges and the Peaches – CHARLES DARWIN (*The Origin of Species*)

Old Lousie and Able Heart – ALEXANDER POPE (*Eloisa to Abelard*)

War on Peas – LEO TOLSTOY (*War and Peace*)

All's Swell That Ends Swell – WILLIAM SHAKESPEARE
(*All's Well That Ends Well*)

Catch One in the Eye – J. D. SALINGER
(*Catcher in the Rye*)

Jason and the Juggernauts (*Jason and the Argonauts*)

Tess of the Dormobiles – THOMAS HARDY
(*Tess of the D'Urbervilles*)

The Mayor of Castersugar – THOMAS HARDY
(*The Mayor of Casterbridge*)

Dangermouse Liaisons – CHODERLOS DE LACLOS
(*Dangerous Liaisons*)

The Lady Ate Shallots – ALFRED, LORD TENNYSON
(*The Lady of Shalott*)

Who so beset him round?

When the writer John Buchan's oldest son, also named John, went to Uganda in 1934 to take up a post as a District Officer with the colonial administration, he was astonished by the degree of joy and excitement that his arrival caused. Perplexed, he turned to one of his new colleagues, who explained, 'These are Christian Africans, educated at mission schools . . . they have come to catch a glimpse of the son of John Bunyan* . . .'

*Author of *The Pilgrim's Progress* – who died in 1688.

Religious Misdirection

Holey Moses

During a phonetics class, tutor John Wells described how his father once told him the Bible story of Moses and the burning bush (Exodus 3):

> 'In the words of the Authorized Version, God spake unto Moses from out of the midst of the bush and said, 'Draw not nigh hither: put off thy shoes from off thy feet, for the place whereon thou standest is holy ground.' But I heard this as hole-y ground, ground with holes in it. If Moses kept his shoes on, I thought, perhaps he would get them caught in the holes.'

Mea culpa

In April 2001, a gentleman told the *Northern Echo* how, in his days as an altar boy, a fellow server had offered the response, 'Me a cowboy, me a cowboy, me a Mexican cowboy.'

Of course, what we are sure he meant to say was 'Mea culpa, mea culpa, mea maxima culpa', which he probably did in the future, as the priest's somewhat unchristian response to the boy's mondegreen was to 'thump him round the lug'.

Mishearing on the mount

In a well-known scene from *Monty Python's Life of Brian* (1979), an argumentative crowd is having trouble hearing the reference to 'peacemakers' while listening to the Sermon on the Mount:

MAN: 'I think it was, "Blessed are the cheesemakers"!'
GREGORY'S WIFE: 'What's so special about the cheesemakers?'
GREGORY: 'Well, obviously it's not meant to be taken literally. It refers to any manufacturers of dairy products.'

God help you, Vicar

VICAR: 'Is everybody here?'
HARD-OF-HEARING LADY in the congregation: 'Yes, perfectly, thank you.'

(From *The Vicar of Dibley*)

VICAR: 'For those of us who are free . . .'
LITTLE GIRL (in congregation): 'I'm four.'

The power of prayer

'The Lord's Prayer' is recited the world over thousands of times a day – so Christians should have got it word-perfect by now, shouldn't they? Here are some lines that strayed from the original version:

'Our Father, with heart in Heaven'

'Our Father Richard in Heaven'

'Our Father Witchart in Heaven'

'Our Father makes art in Heaven'

'Our Father, which art in Heaven, Allah be thy name'

'Our Father, which art in Heaven, Harold be thy name'

'Our Father, who art in Heaven, that will be my name'

'Our Father, who art in Heaven, Howard be thy name'

'Our Father, who art in Heaven, How did you know my name?'

'Give us this day, our gravy and bread'

'Lead us not into Trent station and deliver us from derails'

'*Lead us not into temptation, but deliver us some e-mail*'

'*Forgive us our trash please, as we forgive those who leave trash amongst us*'

'*Deliver us from eagles*'

'*Aunt Leda's not into temptation*'

'*Lead us lot to temptation*'

'*But deliver us from Ealing*'

In Madonna's controversial song 'Like A Prayer', the words 'Let the choir sing' have been misheard as 'Level crossing', while the line 'Just like a muse to me' has been misheard as 'Just like immunity'.

Hail Mary

The 'Hail Mary' or 'Angelic Salutation' is a traditional Catholic prayer. Here follow some less orthodox renditions:
'I remember that we used to say a prayer to Mary in which a monk goes swimming,' recalls one lady. 'The line should have been "Blessed art thou amongst women", but quite a few of us heard it as "Blessed art though, a monk swimming".' She is by no means alone in this mishearing.

'Hail Mary, full of grace'

'Hail Mary, full of grapes'

(Quoted in a recent review of *Girls of Tender Age:
A Memoir* by MARY-ANN TIRONE SMITH)

☆

'Holy Mary, Mother of God, pray for us sinners now,
and at the hour of our death'

*'Holy Mary, Mother of God, pray for our dinners now
and at the hour of our death'*

(Submitted by a good Catholic who describes himself
as having been a hungry child)

☆

'Hail Mary, quite contrary'

(Said by a little girl keen to combine a prayer with a
nursery rhyme)

☆

'Hell Mary, full of grace'

(How many 'Hell Marys' must this unfortunate woman
have said before realizing her error?)

'He suffered under a bunch of spiders'

A mishearing of 'He suffered under Pontius
Pilate', from the Apostles' Creed

Seems we can't Handel this one

At a Portland church years ago, the Reverend Sherman Hesselgrave remembers listening to Handel's *Messiah* but, instead of hearing the words 'Surely he hath borne our griefs,' he heard the somewhat intriguing line, 'Surely he hath worn our briefs.'

There have also been some dubious renditions of this memorable line from Handel's famous work: 'For the Lord God omnipotent reigneth':

'For the Lord God in impudent rages'

'For the Lord God impotent reigneth'

'For the Lord God of nicotine reigneth'

Father, Son, and . . . ?

The Holy Trinity has never sounded so eccentric:

Father, Son and Holy Goat

Father, Son and the whole East Coast

Father Don and the Holy Ghost

Father, Son and the Holy Smoke

Hosanna in excelsis

A father took his son to church, where they sat through a long service. At the end of it, he asked the boy what he thought of the occasion. 'Well, it got a bit better when the priest started talking about Chelsea,' came the reply. Now, the father knew his son was a Chelsea fanatic, and that the football team often clouded his thinking, but he really couldn't understand in this instance to what he was referring.

'You know, the "Hosanna are in Chelsea" bit . . .' the boy explained.

Thanks, Peter God

As a consequence of hearing numerous Bible readings that ended 'Thanks be to God' during school assemblies, one young woman became convinced that God's first name was 'Peter': 'In my childhood innocence, and possibly because of my northern accent, I mistook "be to" for the name "Peter", and concluded that this must be his first name.'

Not unreasonably, she decided that he must have been known as Peter to his close friends.

Hymns Old and New

A s MOST of us learned the words to popular hymns during childhood visits to church, Sunday school or during school assembly, such religious songs offer rich pickings for mondegreens.

Lord of soft furnishings

'Dance then, wherever you may be
I am the Lord of the Dance, said He!
And I'll lead you all, wherever you may be
And I'll lead you all in the Dance, said He!'

When I was at infant school, on one occasion my class-mates and I were encouraged to join in with the above song. Naturally, I sang along with gusto, despite having misheard the second and fourth lines completely, and belted out 'I am the Lord of the dance settee, / And I'll lead you all, wherever you may be / And I'll lead you all to the dance settee.'

Lacking grace

'Amazing grace, how sweet the sound
That saved a wretch like me!
I once was lost, but now am found,
Was blind, but now I see.'

In 1748, John Newton (1725–1807) survived a dangerous storm while he sailed on his slave ship, the *Greyhound*, whereupon he penned the words to what has become the well-loved hymn 'Amazing Grace'. He did not, however, pen the following:

*'I'm ageing great, how sweet thou are
To spare a wretch like me.'*

or indeed . . .

*'Amazing grace, how sweet my aunt
Who saved a wretch like me!'*

or even . . .

*'Amazing grapes, how sweet thou art
To spare some for my tea.'*

or finally . . .

*'Amazing grace, how sweet the sound
That saved a wench like me.'*

Though the first verse is well known for being misheard by many, the third verse has also created confusion. Some have heard the lines 'Through many dangers, toils and snares, I have already come' as 'dangerous toys and dares', 'toys and scares', or even 'toys and snails'.

All things . . .

Cecil Frances Alexander (1818–95) was a prolific writer of hymns, some of which still remain popular to this day. One of her works, written in 1848 and published as 'All Things Bright and Beautiful' in *Hymns for Little Children*, is inexplicably known to some people as 'All Things Brighton Beautiful'.

No angels

In the rousing spiritual song 'Swing Low, Sweet Chariot', the 'band of angels coming after me' referred to in the first verse has occasionally been misinterpreted as a 'band of Indians coming after me . . .'

Onwards and upwards

In 1864, the Reverend Sabine Baring-Gould (1834–1924) knocked out the verses of the processional hymn 'Onward, Christian Soldiers' in about fifteen minutes! He freely admitted that because it was written in such haste, he was 'afraid that some of the rhymes are faulty'. Thus, he was not opposed to revisions of his text, although he might have cause to object to most of these offerings:

ORIGINAL LINE:
'Onward, Christian soldiers, marching as to war'

MONDEGREENS:
'Onward, Christian soldiers, march your ass to war'
'Onward, Christian soldiers, marching out the door'

☆

ORIGINAL LINE:
'With the cross of Jesus going on before'

MONDEGREENS:
'With the cross of Jesus flapping on the floor'
'With the cross-eyed Jesus going on before'
'With the grass of Jesus growing on the floor'

☆

ORIGINAL LINE:
'Christ, the royal Master, leads against the foe'

MONDEGREENS:
'Christ, the royal Master, leads again I know'
'Christ, the royal Master, leans against the phone'

☆

ORIGINAL LINE:
'Forward into battle, see His banners go'

MONDEGREEN:
'Forward into battle, see his bladder flow'

[42]

Moving on to the first line of the third verse of 'Onward, Christian Soldiers' – 'Like a mighty army moves the church of God' – some have been known to sing: 'Like a mighty Auntie moves the church of God.'

Write on, write on

Henry Hart Milman (1791–1868) was an educated chap, who at one time was Poetry Professor at Oxford and later Dean of St Paul's Cathedral in London. In his hymn 'Ride On, Ride On, in Majesty!' the following would not have made the grade:

'Ride on, ride on, to Ma, said he'

'Ride on, ride on, to make my tea'

'Ride on, ride on, to Ma's for tea'

Ham, but no eggs

During the hymn 'There is a Green Hill Far Away' (by Mrs Alexander), a parishioner was overheard singing, 'But we believe it was for us / He had ham supper there' instead of '. . . He hung and suffered there'.

Wrong Diagnoses

'Stan, it's my liver'

A medical mishearing of 'Stand and Deliver'
by Adam and the Ants

Falling behind in med school?

A medical student was rather startled when, during, a CPR (cardiopulmonary resuscitation) class, a fellow student asked him, somewhat apprehensively, 'What's the hind-lick manoeuvre?'

If he wants his medical degree, he had better swot up. Since 1974, when Dr Henry Heimlich introduced his anti-choking abdominal thrust, the procedure is said to have saved more than 100,000 lives, including, it is claimed, those of Cher, Elizabeth Taylor, Goldie Hawn, Carrie Fisher, former President Ronald Reagan, Walter Matthau and Jack Lemmon. More recently, however, some 'experts' have recommended that the Heimlich manoeuvre be used purely as a last resort as it can cause internal injuries. Indeed, Dr Heimlich himself has only had to perform it on one occasion.

The Heimlich manoeuvre has also been mistakenly referred to as the 'Heimlich remover'.

You're winding me up

A doctor who received a wind-up torch as a Christmas present from his mother joked, 'Thanks, it'll be useful on the ward round.'

His mother sniffily replied, 'Well, if you're putting it on the wardrobe, I'll give it to someone who wants one!'

> Did you hear the one about the chap who had a baloney amputation (below-knee amputation)? Or the woman who had a bow-and-arrow test for leukaemia (bone marrow test)? Or the patient who was described as a 'complete cycle-path' (psychopath)?

Women's troubles

A woman of certain age, when asked if her husband was still 'active in that department', replied, 'In the garden? Oh, yes, he's still very active. He mows the lawn twice a week.'

A woman once called her local hospital and asked the receptionist: 'Hello? Can you put me through to Sir Michael Spears?'

What she actually needed was the gynaecology department that dealt with 'cervical smears'.

Meanwhile, another lady misheard 'fibroids of the uterus' as 'fireballs of the Eucharist'.

A young lady recovering from an operation to remove an ovarian cyst was visited by her consultant. He asked her if she wanted children, to which she replied yes. 'Well, then,' said the consultant, 'you should hurry up and get on with it.' But the young lady, to her bemusement, heard '. . . you should just sit on it,' and in surprise asked him – to his mystification – if that was the position he recommended for trying for a baby.

> *'The First Noël, the angels did say,*
> *Was to surgeons for shepherds in fields as they lay'*
>
> A mishearing of the Christmas carol 'The First Noël', in which 'certain poor shepherds' are fêted above surgeons

The 'Jockstrap Position'

A *Times* reader once wrote to the newspaper to tell of a delightful mondegreen perpetrated by the secretary of a renowned physician.

While the doctor was dictating a paper intended for publication in an important medical journal, she misheard the word 'juxtaposition' and bafflingly typed 'jockstrap position' instead. Clearly she had things other than dictation on her mind that afternoon . . .

Easy does it

A three-year-old boy returning from a visit to the circus told his mother that he'd given all his money to the trapeze man. When she asked why, he answered, 'Well, they told us he flies through the air with the greatest disease.'

Pus jewels

Did you know there is a new teenage disease going around? It's called 'pus jewels', and the symptoms are large inflamed spots (pustules).

'Sixty-five roses'

Cystic fibrosis is a life-threatening inherited disease that, sadly, many children are diagnosed with every year. So many of these children have overheard their parents and doctors discussing their disease and believe that they have a disorder called 'sixty-five roses' that the term is now a well-recognized euphemism for the disease.

'Blue Roses'

In *The Glass Menagerie* by Tennessee Williams, the painfully shy character Laura Wingfield reveals that she told the school hero, Jim O'Connor, on whom she had a secret crush, that she missed school due to an attack of 'pleurosis'. Jim mishears the name of the disease, and so begins to call her 'Blue Roses'.

'Oooh, oooh, me ears are alight'

Famous mondegreen of 'Oooh, oooh, the Israelite' from 'The Israelites' by Desmond Dekker and the Aces

---

Cough, cough

An old lady was reluctant to see her doctor about a suspected chest infection, and kept insisting that she was not ill. Eventually, however, she gave in, and was duly given a prescription. When her granddaughter asked her what it was for, she replied 'Antibiollocks'. As her grandmother was not given to swearing, her granddaughter could only assume that it was a slip of the tongue, or that the elderly woman had misheard the doctor prescribing a course of antibiotics.

> 'TB or not TB, that is congestion.'
>
> WOODY ALLEN

'Diarrhoea, here I go again'

Questionable mishearing of 'Mamma Mia, here I go again' from Abba's 'Mamma Mia'

☆

'The girl with colitis goes by'

Famous mishearing of 'the girl with kaleidoscope eyes' from The Beatles' song, 'Lucy in the Sky with Diamonds', otherwise known as 'Lucy and This Guy Are Dying'

'I get hives'

Odd interpretation of the words 'I can't hide' from
The Beatles' 'I Want To Hold Your Hand'

☆

'Leprosy, leprosy, leprosy, leprosy'

Wrong diagnosis of the words to 'Let It Be'
by The Beatles

☆

'Let it bleed, let it bleed, let it bleed, let it bleed'

Another unusual interpretation of 'Let It Be'

☆

'All you bleed is blood'

A mishearing of another Beatles song,
'All You Need Is Love'

☆

'Bring me an iron lung'

A mishearing of 'Bring me a higher love',
from 'Higher Love' by Steve Winwood

☆

'Goodbye, normal genes'

A mishearing of Elton John's tribute to Marilyn Monroe –
'Goodbye, Norma Jean' – from 'Candle in the Wind'

Ignorance
Isn't Always Bliss

'A stupid man's report of what a clever man says can never be accurate, because he unconsciously translates what he hears into something he can understand.'

BERTRAND RUSSELL (1872–1970)

Not something to crow about

Perhaps more of a misreading or misinterpretation than an actual mishearing, this story from the Knight Ridder News Service is nevertheless worth noting.

After receiving the letter below, the US Department of the Interior decided it was time to change the inscription on the metal bands used to tag migratory birds. The bands had used to bear the address of the Washington Biological Survey, abbreviated Wash. Biol. Surv., until an Arkansas camper sent the agency the following note:

Dear Sirs:
While camping last week I shot one of your birds. I think it was a crow. I followed the cooking instructions on the leg tag and I want to tell you it was horrible.

The bands are now marked 'Fish and Wildlife Service'.

Boom boom

A first-time female sailor ended up with a swollen nose and a cold dip in the sea, when she embarked on her maiden sailing trip on a small and overcrowded boat. Knowing nothing of boating terminology, when the helmsman suddenly shouted 'Ready about, lee-ho!' she assumed he was addressing someone in the boat named Leo. She didn't notice everyone else duck out of the way, and got a nasty surprise when the boom hit her across her nose, the force of which carried her out of the boat and into the Solent. 'Since then, I can assure you I have always been "Ready about",' she said.

DEL: 'One of my most favouritest meals is Duck à l'Orange, but I don't know how to say that in French.'
RODNEY: 'It's *canard*.'
DEL: 'You can say that again, bruv!'
RODNEY: 'No, the French word for duck is *canard*.'
DEL: 'Is it? I thought that was something to do with the *QE2*?'
RODNEY: 'No, that's Cunard.'

From *Only Fools & Horses*,
'Strangers on the Shore' (2002)

Law and Disorder

Taking the Flack . . .

The words to the song 'Killing Me Softly' (made famous by Roberta Flack) have caused problems for quite a few listeners. The singer has been killed softly with 'insoles', 'insults' and 'incense', as well as 'his song'.

Arson it wasn't . . .

'Terrible that business. Did you know our son was involved?'

'I didn't know they set fire to the house as well.'

'They didn't.'

Am I hearing you right?

A policeman recently rang a nurse to discuss the details of the theft of her purse: 'I'm calling to talk about your snatch.' The line was not too good. 'My sn . . . ? Sorry, *what* did you say, officer?'

Put a cork in it

A noisy pub provided the background to this mishearing.

First drinker: 'I won't have another; I'm going to Cork tomorrow.'
Fellow drinker: 'Really? What for?'
First drinker (laughing): 'A stag weekend.'
Fellow drinker: 'My God, what did you get up to?'
First drinker: 'Um . . . No, I'm going tomorrow.'
Fellow drinker: 'Yeah, you said you're going to court.
I want to know what you got up to on that stag weekend.'
First drinker: '*Cork*! I'm going to Cork, *not* court!'
Fellow drinker (disappointed): 'Oh.'

Cat bungler

An Internet blog tells the fantastical tale of a potentially unfortunate mishearing – unfortunate for the animal involved, at any rate.

In short, a bunch of hoodlums had tied a man to a chair, and after having slapped and threatened their victim without getting what they want from him, the 'boss gangsta' became impatient and instructed one of his henchmen to 'Pop a cap in his ass, yo' (i.e. shoot him in the rear). The chosen lackey gave his boss a confused look and told him, 'But I ain't got no cat.' However, the boss had no time for such equivocation, so the man went off disconsolately and eventually reappeared clutching a cat.

Fortunately, in the ensuing fracas both the moggie and the intended victim escape, the cat managing to avoid what must surely be described as a fate worse than death.

Tardy transcription

In a letter to *The Times*, the writer and former BBC broadcaster Sir Antony Jay described a mondegreen arising from the transcription of one of the BBC's live broadcast talks: 'I once said: "To quote Clough, 'Say not the struggle naught availeth'," and found it transcribed as: "To quote fluff, 'Up the struggle naughty bailiff'."'

Actual bodily harm

According to one Carpenters fan, for years she had misheard the line 'Breaking each other's heart' from 'Hurting Each Other' as 'Breaking each other's arm'.

Actual bodily harm

A gentlemen misheard 'Bennie and the Jets' by Elton John as 'Beat Me in the Chest', while a lady thought the Creedence Clearwater Revival song 'I Put a Spell on You' (also sung by Nina Simone) was 'I'm Going to Spit on You'. Finally, some misguided person heard the opening words to Abba's 'Chiquitita' – 'Chiquitita, tell me what's wrong . . .' – as 'Kick her teeth out, tell me what's wrong . . .'.

Just what was ordered . . .

After a day's training, forty lawyers from an assortment of offices of an international law firm enjoyed dinner on a boat on Amsterdam's canals, and, following a tour of several bars, the hard core among them ended up in a disco.

One of the hosts kindly offered to buy the next round, and asked an English delegate what he should get. 'Sambucas would be good,' came the reply.

'How many?' responded the generous local lawyer, shouting above the general din of the establishment.

'Oh, I think ten should be sufficient.'

About twenty minutes later, the two bumped into each other.

'Sambucas?'

'Oh, they should be here any minute.'

'Are they being brought over to us?'

'Well, I don't know how they are getting here.'

This prompted a puzzled look, and a pause, before the host continued a little nervously: 'You did ask for some hookers, *ja*?'

A small matter of legalities

A Scottish solicitor and notary public revealed to a national newspaper that he once received a letter addressed to 'Solicitor and not a republic'.

Lost in transcription

The Los Angeles Times published these examples of tapes that were badly transcribed:

☆ Traders & General Insurance Company was referred to as 'Traitors and General'.

☆ The legalism 'as aforestated' came out as 'as Alfred stated'.

☆ A line that was supposed to read: 'The conduct of plaintiff is egregious and warrants the imposition of sanctions' became 'the imposition of venison'.

A breathy debriefing

Also reported in *The Los Angeles Times*, a reader told the story of a marketing manager from Boston who, on his return from a factory visit in a foreign country, dictated a memo to a colleague that was copied to the rest of the department. The memo contained an intriguing request: 'Please attend a deep-breathing meeting tomorrow morning.'

Sharp shooters

'I Shot the Sheriff' by Bob Marley (also sung by Eric Clapton) has thrown up countless mondegreens on all manner of subjects:

MISHEARINGS:

'I shot the sheriff, but I didn't shoot him dead you see'

'I shot the sheriff, but I did not shoot the dead beauty'

'I shot the sheriff, but I did not shoot the dead pony'

'I shopped with Cheryl . . .'

'I shot the sherry . . .'

Modern Malapropisms

> 'It is the disease of not listening, the malady of not marking, that I am troubled withal.'
>
> FALSTAFF, *King Henry IV, Part 2*

post-traumatic stress disorder
post-*dramatic* stress disorder

two cents' worth
two *sense* worth

the human genome project
the human *gnome* project

the judicial and penal system
the judicial and *penile* system

a cappuccino
a *cup of chino*

hand-me-downs
hammy-downs

polka-dotted
poke-a-dotted

the underlying principles
the *underlining* principles

last vestiges of fun and merriment
last *vestibules* of fun and merriment

we were in the midst of it
we were in the *mist* of it

she was flabbergasted
she was *fibregasted*

it's like an albatross around my neck
it's like an *Alcatraz* around my neck

kowtowing to the powers that be
cow towing to the powers that be

in a fraction of a second
in a *fracture* of a second

given up the ghost
given up the *goat*

I did it off my own bat
I did it off my own *back*

she's got another think coming
she's got another *thing* coming

'There are nine million bison in Beijing'

A mishearing of Katie Melua's 'Nine Million
Bicycles in Beijing'

Festive Mishearings

CHRISTMAS SONGS seem to lend themselves to an abundance of mishearings. Possibly this is because we learned so many of them as children, when our vocabularies were still unsophisticated, and our parents were too enchanted by our delightful renditions of 'Away in a Manger' and 'Rudolph the Red-Nosed Reindeer' to set us straight. Whatever our reasons for belting out the wrong words at Christmas time, the following festive mondegreens should brighten the spirits at any time of the year.

Mistidings of comfort and joy ...

'God Rest Ye Merry, Gentlemen' is one of our oldest carols with lyrics dating back to the fifteenth century. It is thought that it was sung to the gentry by town watchmen to earn additional money during the Christmas season.

Since the carol was first penned, however, numerous misinterpretations have been made:

ORIGINAL LINE:

'God rest ye merry, gentlemen, let nothing you dismay'

MONDEGREENS:

'God rest ye merry, gentlemen, let nothing you display'

'Get dressed, ye married gentlemen, you must have done with May'

'Give rest unmarried gentlemen from weddings due in May'

☆

ORIGINAL LINE:

'To save us all from Satan's power when we were gone astray'

MONDEGREEN:

'To save us all from sacred cows when they are gone astray'

☆

One gentleman recalls that he once heard some of the boys at his school singing 'God rest ye Jerry mentalmen'. As he was then not sophisticated enough to observe the deliberate spoonerism, he trustingly sang these words until his housemaster put him straight on the matter.

It is likely that the originators of the 'Jerry mentalmen' were front-line soldiers during the First World War, the words a jibe at the German enemy.

One confused infant seemed to have got Father Christmas mixed up with the Devil, as he was heard singing 'To save us all from *Santa's* power'.

☆

A final word on this carol comes from a woman who, until recently, believed that the opening line of this carol was, 'God rest ye, merry gentlemen', with the comma following 'ye' rather than 'merry'.

She had assumed that the men in question were being advised to take a bit of a break after a lengthy spell of merry-making. In fact, when the hymn was written, the word 'rest' meant 'keep' and 'merry' meant 'strong' or 'mighty', so the title actually means 'May God keep you gentlemen strong,' not 'Put your feet up, you pissheads.'

Not quite so faithful to the original . . .

An author who spent part of her childhood in Japan admits to having misunderstood the words to the carol 'O Come, All Ye Faithful':

> As a child, I lived in a village called Okamoto. We also had a housekeeper of the same name. At Christmas, I was heard singing 'O-*kam*-oto faithful . . .'. They thought I meant the village, but in fact I had the housekeeper in mind.

The Good King's Lass

Wenceslas I was the Prince (Duke) of Bohemia in the tenth century, until he was assassinated by his brother Boleslaw and his followers. He is most famously mentioned in the eponymous Christmas carol, though its lyrics have given rise to many confusions over the years.

ORIGINAL LINE:

'Good King Wenceslas looked out, on the feast of Stephen'

MONDEGREENS:

'Good King Wence's lass looked out, on the feast of Stephen'

'Good King Wences last looked out, on the feast of Stephen'

'Good King Wenches last looked out, on the feast of Stephen'

'Good King Wenceslas looked out, on a piece of Stephen'

'Good King Wences' car backed out, on the feet of heathens'

Angels sung with relish

From the nineteenth-century carol 'Angels from the Realms of Glory' by James Montgomery, some listeners are said to have picked up on a reference to God's apparent penchant for egg-based dressings.

ORIGINAL LINE:
'God with man is now residing'

MONDEGREEN:
'God with mayonnaise residing'

'Round John virgin's motherless child'

A youthful mishearing of
'Round yon Virgin Mother and Child'

Astray from the manger

'Away in a Manger' (or Luther's Cradle Hymn) was originally published in 1885 in a Lutheran Sunday-school book, though its author is unknown. Famous for bringing tears to the eyes of proud parents during Christmas concerts and nativity plays, the carol has also thrown up a host of unusual alternative renditions:

ORIGINAL LINE:
'Away in a manger'

MONDEGREENS:
'A Wayne in a manger'

'A wean in a manger'
('wean' is a Scottish word for 'baby')

ORIGINAL LINE:
'No crib for a bed'

MONDEGREENS:
'No crisps in his bed'
'No creep in the bed'

ORIGINAL LINE:
'The little Lord Jesus laid down His sweet head'

MONDEGREENS:
'The little Lord Cheezits lay down His sweet head'
'The little Lord Jesus lay down His wee ted'

ORIGINAL LINE:
'The little Lord Jesus asleep on the hay'

MONDEGREENS:
'The little Lord Jesus was eating the hay'
'The little Lord Jesus asleep in the shed'

ORIGINAL LINE:
'The cattle are lowing, the baby awakes'

MONDEGREEN:

'The cattle are blowing the baby away'

Recalling the effects of wartime rationing on the mind of a child desperate for chocolate, one person came up with her own unique take on the first verse:

'Away in a manger, no crib for a bed,
The little Malteser laid down its sweet head.
The stars in the bright sky looked down where it lay.
That little Malteser, asleep on the hay.'

Thieving baby Jesus

After hearing 'Little Jesus, Sweetly Sleep' (known as 'The Rocking Carol') for the first time, one small child got a little bit confused. Instead of singing 'We will rock you, rock you, rock you . . .' he was overheard belting out: 'He will rob you, rob you, rob you . . .'

TEACHER: 'Children, why are Mary and Joseph travelling to Bethlehem?'
CHILD: 'To pay for the taxis.'

Mother and baby

'My daughter got me into an embarrassing situation once. For days she had been singing, "Mummy's having a baby, yes good" and so I had wondered if it was a song they sang at her nursery. I didn't give it much more thought until two of the teachers and a couple of mothers asked me when my baby was due.

'As I had just had my second child, with a fairly short gap between that one and the first, I couldn't imagine why anyone would expect me to be pregnant again. The matter was cleared up when I attended my daughter's nativity play, when the children in her group stood and sang, "Mary's having a baby, yes Lord . . ."'

Please may we have peas?

'Silent night, holy night,
All is calm, all is bright.
Round yon Virgin Mother and Child,
Holy Infant so tender and mild.
Sleep in heavenly peace,
Sleep in heavenly peace.'

'Silent Night', the well-known Christmas hymn by Father Josef Mohr and Franz Grüber, has been the subject of numerous different mishearings. Following on from the original first verse above comes a mondegreen extraordinaire:

'Solid night, hold me tight,
All is calm, all is bright.
Brown young virgin, mother hen child,
Holy "infantso" tender and mild.
Sleep in heavenly peas,
Sleep in heavenly peas.'

Come meet John Virgin

One *Los Angeles Times* reader told how his late aunt, an elementary schoolteacher, always liked to tell the tale of a kindergarten pupil who, while on a trip to see Father Christmas, asked: 'Which one is Santa and which one is Round John Virgin?'

Not sure about this Santa person

While waiting for the arrival of the great man in red, some small children would appear to have got a bit carried away when singing 'Santa Claus is Coming to Town'.

ORIGINAL LINE:

'Santa Claus is coming to town!'

MONDEGREEN:

'Santa Claus is mowing my lawn!'

[69]

ORIGINAL LINE:

'He's making a list, he's checking it twice'

MONDEGREEN:

'He's making a list and chicken and rice'

☆

ORIGINAL LINE:

'He's gonna find out who's naughty or nice'

MONDEGREEN:

'He's gonna find out who's snoring at night'

☆

ORIGINAL LINE:

'He sees you when you're sleeping'

MONDEGREEN:

'He'll seize you when you're sleeping'

Not sure about that Jack Frost, either

As far of most of us are concerned, in 'The Christmas Song' ('Chestnuts Roasting on an Open Fire') by Torme and Wells, little, furry animals are definitely not being sacrificed in a yard fire . . .

ORIGINAL LINE:
'Chestnuts roasting on an open fire'

MONDEGREEN:
'Chipmunks roasting on an open fire'
'Chest hairs roasting on an open fire'
'Chestnuts boasting on an open fire'

ORIGINAL LINE:
'Jack Frost nipping on your nose'

MONDEGREEN:
'Jack Frost ripping off your clothes'

ORIGINAL LINE:
'And folks dressed up like Eskimos'

MONDEGREEN:
'And folks dressed up like escaroles'

'I'm cleaning out a white grease mess'

Frank Muir's interpretation of 'I'm dreaming of a white Christmas'

What fresh hell

'The First Noël' is thought to date back to the sixteenth century. Plenty of time to get the lyrics in a muddle, then, as we can see from the following offerings:

ORIGINAL LINES:

'The First Noël, the Angels did say,
Was to certain poor shepherds in fields as they lay'

MONDEGREEN:

'The First Noël, the Angels did say,
Was to serve them poor shepherds, in fields where they lay'

☆

ORIGINAL LINE:
'Noël, Noël, Noël, Noël'

MONDEGREENS:
'No hell, no hell, no hell, no hell'
'Oh well, oh well, oh well, oh well'
'No elves, no elves, no elves'

☆

ORIGINAL LINE:
'Born is the King of Israel!'

MONDEGREEN:
'Barney's the King of Israel!'

Those troublesome elves

'Last Christmas, as I was playing "I spy" with my six-year-old, I realized that her turn seemed to be going on for ever. She told me that the word was something to do with Christmas and it began with "N". I looked and looked and racked my brains, but finally had to admit defeat.

'Finally, tired of my ineptitude, she revealed, "It's a nelf, silly."'

Deck the halls with . . .

The music to 'Deck the Halls' is believed to be Welsh in origin and was reputed to have come from a tune called 'Nos Galan' dating back to the sixteenth century, while the words are said to have originated in nineteenth-century America.

Instead of decking the halls with 'boughs of holly', however, some people have occasionally favoured strange alternatives, including 'Buddy Holly' and 'parts of Molly'.

Wilting in a winter wonderland

The Christmas song 'Winter Wonderland' was first published in 1934 and was popularly recorded by the Andrews

Sisters and Perry Como. The lyrics famously conjure up the perfect Christmas scene – that snowy, wintry landscape. Or do they? Here are some mishearings that might suggest that things have warmed up a little:

'In the meadow we can build a snowman,
Then pretend that he is *parched and brown*'
(Parson Brown)

'Later on, we'll *perspire as we sit* by the fire'
('Later on, we'll conspire as we dream by the fire')

'Walking in our winter *underwear*'
('Walking in our winter wonderland')

Piggy pudding, anyone?

As you gather with friends and family to celebrate the joys of Yuletide, singing the well-known song 'We Wish You A Merry Christmas', listen out for any choice misinterpretations of its second verse in particular.

ORIGINAL LINE:

'Now bring us some figgy pudding'

MONDEGREEN:

'Now bring us some friggin' pudding'
'Now bring us a piggy pudding'

'Good tidings we bring, to you and your kin'

MONDEGREEN:

'Good tidings we bring, to you and your king'

Hark, what did the herald angels sing?

Written by Charles Wesley in 1742, 'Hark! The Herald Angels Sing' is one of the most rousing Christmas hymns ever written. Pity, then, that while some people are bellowing it out from the congregation, they're making a complete hash of the lyrics . . .

ORIGINAL LINE:

'Hark! the herald angels sing'

MONDEGREENS:

'Hark the hair-lipped angels sing'

'Hark the herald agency'

'Hark the Harold angels sing'

'Hartley Hare the angels sing'

(a reference to the British children's TV programme
Pipkins, which ran from 1973 to 1981,
and featured Hartley Hare)

ORIGINAL LINE:
'Glory to the newborn King!'

MONDEGREEN:
'Glory to the New York King!'

☆

ORIGINAL LINE:
'God and sinners reconciled'

MONDEGREENS:
'God and sinners wreck your smiles'
'God and sinners wrecked a child'
'God and sinners quite reviled'
'Garden centres wreck a child'

☆

ORIGINAL LINE:
'With the angelic host proclaim'

MONDEGREEN:
'With the jelly toast proclaim'

Who's calling whom names?

In 1939, advertising executive Robert May was commissioned to write a Christmas poem for children visiting a department store. It proved so popular that 2.5 million copies were handed out in its first year of publication. That poem became the Christmas song 'Rudolph, the Red-Nosed Reindeer', but despite its popularity some of us still can't help tripping up over particular lines.

ORIGINAL LINE:

'All of the other reindeer . . .'

MONDEGREENS:

'Adolf, the other reindeer . . .'

'Olive, the other reindeer . . .'

ORIGINAL LINES:

'Rudolph the red-nosed reindeer,
You'll go down in history!'

MONDEGREENS:

*'Rudolph the red-nosed reindeer,
You'll go down in his story!'*

*'Rudolph the red-nosed reindeer,
You'll go down and hit the tree!'*

Jingle on . . .

One of the most famous American Christmas songs is 'Jingle Bells'. Written in 1857 by minister James Pierpoint, you'd think we'd be able to get the words right by now, but surprisingly, most of us only really know the chorus . . .

ORIGINAL LINE:

'Dashing through the snow in a one-horse open sleigh'

MONDEGREENS:

'Dashing through the snow in a one-horse soapen sleigh'

'Dashing through the snow in a one-horse Chevrolet'

'Dashing through the snow in a one-horse soap and sleigh'

ORIGINAL LINE:

'Bells on bobtails ring'

MONDEGREEN:

'Bells on cocktails ring'

ORIGINAL LINES:

'Bells on bobtails ring, making spirits bright
What fun it is to laugh and sing a sleighing song tonight'

MONDEGREEN:

*'Bells on Bob's tail ring, making spareribs bright
What fun it is to write and sing a slaying song to knives'*

A bum note . . .

The much-loved hymn 'We Three Kings' was written in 1857 by the Reverend John Henry Hopkins. Misreadings of its lyrics have thrown up countless bizarre mondegreens . . .

ORIGINAL LINE:

'We three kings of Orient are'

MONDEGREENS:

'We three kings of porridge and tar'

'We free kings of Oregon are'

'We three kings from Orient tar'

ORIGINAL LINE:

'Bearing gifts we trav'rse afar'

MONDEGREEN:

'Burying gifts we travel so far'

ORIGINAL LINE:

'Glorious, now behold him arise'

MONDEGREEN:

'Glorious, now behold haemorrhoids'

The end is nigh

Finally, regarding the original German version of 'O Christmas Tree', one just has to ask whether the person who claims he sang 'O atom bomb, O atom bomb' instead of 'O Tannenbaum, O Tannenbaum' was really entering into the Christmas spirit.

National Anthems and Patriotic Hiccups

NATIONAL ANTHEMS and patriotic songs are sensitive subjects at the best of times, with many people feeling that they need a little reworking, whether it is to remove the reference to 'Rebellious Scots' from a verse in the British national anthem, or to translate 'The Star-Spangled Banner' into Spanish – to say nothing of various football chants. Here follows just a few examples.

Those pesky Victorians

In its original incarnation of 'God Save the King', this patriotic song was first performed in 1745 in London. When Queen Victoria and Queen Elizabeth II acceded to the throne, naturally the British public had to remember to sing 'God Save the Queen', and most of them did, except for the odd exception:

ORIGINAL LINE:

'God save our gracious Queen'

MONDEGREEN:

'God shave our gracious Queen'

☆

ORIGINAL LINES:

'Send her victorious,
Happy and glorious'

MONDEGREEN:

*'Send them Victorians,
Happily boring us'*

Land of hope . . .

'Land of Hope and Glory,
Mother of the Free,
How shall we extol thee,
Who are born of thee?'

This rousing patriotic song by Edward Elgar (music) and
Arthur C. Benson (words) has often thrown up various
different mondegreens, including 'Mother of the three /
How shall we ignore thee' and 'Who was it that stole thee /
Who are born of thee?'

And listening to a class of school children singing this
recently, a parent noticed they all sang 'ex-story' rather
than 'extol thee'.

A Soldier's Song

In an extract from Irish newspaper *The Corkman*, a contributor described his own misunderstanding of the lyrics of the Irish national anthem, 'A Soldier's Song' or 'Amhán Na bhFiann'. He had been at a sports event as a child when he overheard a man singing the national anthem in the Irish language.

As a result, he became convinced that the last line was 'Shoving Connie around the green', and it wasn't until his teenage years that he realized the correct line was 'Seo Libh canaidh amhrán na bhFiann', which translates into English as 'We'll sing a soldier's song.'

I pledge a, ah, ah . . .

The USA's 'Pledge of Allegiance' was devised in 1892, partly to celebrate the 400th anniversary of Columbus's arrival in the Americas. Some proud US citizens haven't always heard the solemn words correctly, however, and come up with a few strange phrases instead:

ORIGINAL LINE:

'I pledge allegiance to the flag . . .'

MONDEGREENS:

'I pledge a lesion to the flag . . .'

'*I led the pigeons to the flag . . .*'

'*I pledge a lesson to the frog . . .*'

☆

ORIGINAL LINES:

'And to the Republic for which it stands,
One Nation, under God, indivisible'

MONDEGREENS:

'*And to the republic for Richard Stans
Once naked, under God, in the vestibule*'

'*And to the republic for Richard Sands
One Asian, under God, in a dirigible*'

'*And to the republic for witches' dance
One potion, under guard, invisible*'

☆

ORIGINAL LINE:

'With liberty and justice for all'

MONDEGREEN:

'*With liver tea and dresses for all*'

'*With Libby's tea and just us four small*'

'*With little tea and just rice for all*'

That marred and tangled banner . . .

In 1814, the poet Francis Scott Key was celebrating the American victory over the British when he wrote the poem 'Defence of Fort McHenry', which later became known as 'The Star-Spangled Banner' and officially became the USA's national anthem in 1931. Mishearings of the words to this rousing song appear to be rife, however. Here are some examples:

ORIGINAL LINE:

'O say, can you see, by the dawn's early light'

MONDEGREENS:

'José, can you see, by the dawn's early light'

'O say, can you see, by the danzaly light'

ORIGINAL LINE:

'Whose broad stripes and bright stars, through the perilous fight'

MONDEGREEN:

'Who brought stripes and fried stars, through the barrel of Sprite'

ORIGINAL LINE:

'O'er the ramparts we watched . . .'

MONDEGREEN:

'O, the red parts we washed . . .'

☆

ORIGINAL LINE:

'O'er the land of the free and the home of the brave?'

MONDEGREENS:

'O'er the land of the free and the home of the Braves?'

'Or the lamb of the free and the home of the brave?'

America the Beautiful

Written by Katherine Lee Bates in 1895, 'America the Beautiful' is a patriotic song that is almost as highly regarded as the US national anthem. But its proud singers still don't always know the correct words:

ORIGINAL LINE:

'O beautiful, for spacious skies'

MONDEGREEN:

'Oh beautiful, for spaceship skies'

☆

ORIGINAL LINE:

'America! America!
God shed His grace on Thee'

MONDEGREEN:

*'America! America!
God shared His grapes with me'*

☆

ORIGINAL LINE:

'And crown Thy good with brotherhood'

MONDEGREENS:

'And crown Thy good Red Riding Hood'
'And crown Thy good with Robin Hood'

☆

ORIGINAL LINE:

'From sea to shining sea'

MONDEGREEN:

'From sea to Chinese Sea'

The last line may be a sticking point

In 1832, 'My Country 'Tis of Thee', unofficially known as 'America', was written within half an hour on a bit of scrap paper by the Reverend Samuel F. Smith.

Used as a national anthem for much of the nineteenth century, certain individuals managed to mishear the last line of the first verse – 'From every mountainside let freedom ring' – as 'From every mountainside let free the meringue.'

God bless the US of A

Another American patriotic song, 'God Bless America', was originally penned by Irving Berlin in 1918, and revised twenty years later as a peace song at a time when Adolf Hitler was growing ever more powerful in Europe.

Numerous mondegreens arose from Berlin's lyrics, including 'While the storm clouds gather far across the sea, / Let us *wear our Lee Jeans*' (instead of 'Let us swear allegiance') and 'God bless America, land that I love / Stand beside her and guide her / Through the night with the light *from a bulb*' (instead of 'from above').

La Malaise

In the French national anthem, 'La Marseillaise', one common mishearing of a line is 'The Vienna Jews could don no bra', which in French is 'Ils viennent jusque dans nos bras.'

Advance Australia Less Fair

The offical anthem of Australia is 'Advance Australia Fair'. Composed by Peter Dodds McCormick in the 1870s, it did not become the nation's official anthem until 1984.

The first two lines, 'Australians all let us rejoice / For we are young and free' have been sung in many erroneous ways:

*'Australians all own ostriches
Four minus one is three'*

*'Australians all let us be boys
For we are young and three'*

*'Australians let us all meet Joyce
For she is young and free'*

*'Australians all eat ostriches
For we are young at three'*

*'Australians all eat sausages
For we are young and free'*

Making a Meal of It

M ANY MISHEARINGS seem to involve food . . . probably
when our appetite gets the better of our brains.

'His mother served up artichokes.'

'"Auntie choked," did you say?'

Fair dealing

'Are you going to starve an old friend?' or 'Are you going
to start an affair?' are well-known mondegreens of the
opening line of 'Scarborough Fair/Canticle' – 'Are you
going to Scarborough Fair?' Famously recorded by Simon
and Garfunkel, it was the title track of their 1966 album
Parsley, Sage, Rosemary and Thyme, and was later included
on the soundtrack to *The Graduate.*

***

'Family tea breeds contempt'

GRAFFITO inspired by Aesop's saying
'Familiarity breeds contempt'

***

Beer anyone?

'Well I woke up this morning and got myself a beer'

According to Doors member Ray Manzarek, in 'Roadhouse Blues' Jim Morrison was in fact singing 'Well I woke up this morning and I got myself a beard.'

Your lunch has legs

'You don't mind if I move this centrepiece, do you?' a dinner guest asked, indicating a rather tall flower arrangement on the table. 'It's in the way of the talking this end of the table.'

To everyone's astonishment another guest leapt up and backed away from the table, knocking over her chair and shouting, 'A centipede! A centipede walking on the table!'

Staying on the subject of lunch and legs, a somewhat rotund young lady asked her gym instructor: 'How did you achieve those fantastic legs?'

The instructor's answer surprised her.

'Really? Plenty of lunches?' the young woman questioned.

'That would be nice, wouldn't it?' the instructor replied, 'only I said "lunges".'

Singers or Sinners

A churchgoer recalled that the Sunday-school treat in her parish involved a trip out, a lot of eating and the singing of hymns during the return journey. The children would happily belt out, 'We can sing, full though we be,' rather subverting the original 'Weak and sinful though we be.'

Singing for your supper:
some foody mishearings

ORIGINAL:
'You ain't nothin' but a hound dog'

MISHEARING:
'You ate nothing but a hot dog'
(Elvis Presley, 'Hound Dog')

☆

ORIGINAL:
'Sweet dreams are made of this'

MISHEARING:
'Sweet dreams are made of cheese'
(Eurythmics, 'Sweet Dreams')

ORIGINAL:
'I am a rock, I am an island'

MISHEARING:
'I am a rock, I am an onion'
(Simon and Garfunkel, 'I am a Rock')

☆

ORIGINAL:
'Forever Young'

MISHEARING:
'Filet Mignon'
(Bob Dylan, 'Forever Young')

☆

ORIGINAL:
'Taking care of business'

MISHEARING:
'Baking carrot biscuits'
(Bachman-Turner Overdrive,
'Taking Care of Business')

☆

ORIGINAL:
'I'll never be your beast of burden'

MISHEARING:
'I'll never see your pizza burnin''
(The Rolling Stones,
'Beast of Burden')

ORIGINAL:
'Spare him his life from this monstrosity'

MISHEARING:
'Spare him his life for his four sausages'
(Queen, 'Bohemian Rhapsody')

☆

ORIGINAL:
'Last night I dreamt of San Pedro'

MISHEARING:
'Last night I dreamt of some bagels'
(Madonna, 'La Isla Bonita')

☆

ORIGINAL:
'I am a material girl'

MISHEARING:
'I am a cereal girl'
(Madonna, 'Material Girl')

☆

ORIGINAL:
'Take a chance on me'

MISHEARING:
'Take a chunk of meat'
(Abba, 'Take a Chance on Me')

Original:
'Papa don't preach'

Mishearing:
'Poppadom preach'
(Madonna, 'Papa Don't Preach')

☆

Original:
'Red, red wine,
Stay close to me'

Mishearing:
*'Red, red wine,
Steak, lobster, meat'*
(UB40, 'Red, Red Wine')

☆

Original:
'She's got a ticket to ride'

Mishearing:
'She's having chicken tonight'
(The Beatles, 'Ticket to Ride')

☆

Original:
'Swallowed all my pride'

Mishearing:
'Swallowed all my fries'
(Madonna, 'Beautiful Stranger')

ORIGINAL:
'Don't it make my brown eyes blue'

MISHEARING:
'Doughnuts make my brown eyes blue'
(Crystal Gayle,
'Don't it Make My Brown Eyes Blue')

☆

ORIGINAL:
'There's a pawn shop on the corner'

MISHEARING:
'There's a pork chop on the counter'
(Guy Mitchell,
'Pittsburgh, Pennsylvania')

☆

ORIGINAL:
'Holiday, celebrate!'

MISHEARING:
'Hollandaise, salivate!'
(Madonna, 'Holiday')

☆

ORIGINAL:
'Chiquitita, tell me what's wrong . . .'

MISHEARING:
'Chicken tikka, tell me what's wrong . . .'
(Abba, 'Chiquitita')

ORIGINAL:
'I miss you like crazy'

MISHEARING:
'I miss you like gravy'
(Natalie Cole,
'Miss You Like Crazy')

☆

ORIGINAL:
'I wanna be sedated'

MISHEARING:
'I want a piece of bacon'
(The Ramones,
'I Wanna Be Sedated')

☆

ORIGINAL:
'A mulatto, an albino, a mosquito, my libido'

MISHEARING:
'A mulatto, an albino, a mosquito, a burrito'
(Nirvana, 'Smells Like Teen Spirit')

☆

ORIGINAL:
'Here we are now, entertain us'

MISHEARING:
'Here we are now, mashed potatoes'
(Nirvana, 'Smells Like Teen Spirit')

ORIGINAL:
'It's a heartache'

MISHEARING:
'It's a hard egg'
(Bonnie Tyler, 'It's a Heartache')

☆

ORIGINAL:
'Spare him his life from this monstrosity'

MISHEARING:
'Spare him his life for a strong cup of tea'
(Queen, 'Bohemian Rhapsody')

☆

ORIGINAL:
'Cold, cold heart'

MISHEARING:
'Cocoa heart'
(Elton John, 'Sacrifice')

'Les Français adore the pee at door'
'Les Français abhorrent Le Piat d'Or'

'Les Français adore Le Piat d'Or'
– advertising slogan for a brand of wine

Hamming it up

In the late 1960s, a group of fifteen-year-old schoolboys set off for a camping holiday in France, and were driven by one of their mothers to Dover to catch the ferry. As a liberal-minded individual, it occurred to her that the boys might well enjoy their first sexual experiences during their holiday, and so she tried to give the lads a handful of contraceptives to take with them. Utterly embarrassed by the gesture, the lads firmly refused.

Arriving at the ferry terminal they all climbed out, gathered their kit, and said relieved goodbyes. However, as they walked away, the mother felt it her duty to try one last time to press some protection upon the young men. 'Are you sure you don't want any French letters?' she called after them. One of the boys, however, misheard her last two words as 'frankfurters', and shouted back cheerily, 'No thanks – we've got a pound of ham,' leaving the well-meaning woman in a state of complete bewilderment.

Out of the frying pan

In *World Wide Word* by Michael Quinion, the author recalled a song from his youth called 'Shrimp Boats', which was popular in the 1950s. It featured the line 'The shrimp boats are a-coming, their sails are in sight', but for more than forty years the author had been convinced that the second half of the line was 'they'll be frying tonight', which wasn't unreasonable, really.

Cheesy request

Strange but true, a patron at an Italian restaurant was overheard asking for 'Farmer John cheese' instead of the more traditional Parmesan variety.

Pasta please, pastor

A small boy attending Mass surprised fellow worshippers one Sunday, when, instead of singing 'Hosanna, in the highest', he came out with 'Lasagna, in the highest.'

Eggs Benedict – or near enough

A couple was staying at a B&B and had just sat down to breakfast. The waitress asked them if they would like a cooked breakfast, and if so how would they like their eggs? The husband, in an effort to be obliging, replied that he would have them however they came. A few minutes later, the waitress popped her head round the door and announced: 'The Pope's dead.'

'Poached eggs are fine,' responded her guest.

Sounds fishy to me . . .

A lady had just returned from a trip to see her brother in Perth, Australia. She was excitedly describing a visit to the Margaret River, when someone across the table asked if there was still a bad drought in that part of the world. '"Bad trout?" Oh, no, I don't think they have those Down Under.' (Actually, they do have trout, good ones.)

Trapped

Continuing with the fishing theme, another lady admits to being haunted by a misapprehension that the words to Elvis Presley's 'Suspicious Minds' were 'We're calling a trout,' instead of the more obvious, 'We're caught in a trap.'

That's Not My Number

―――

ACTUAL LYRIC:
'I'm too sexy for my shirt'

MISHEARING:
'It's two-sixty for my shirt' [£2.60]
(Right Said Fred, 'I'm Too Sexy')

☆

ACTUAL LYRIC:
'She's got Bette Davis eyes'

MISHEARING:
'She's got thirty days to die'
(Kim Carnes, 'Bette Davis Eyes')

☆

*'You picked a fine time to leave me, Lucille,
Four hundred children and a crop in the field'*

There are 'Four hungry children' in Kenny Rogers's
'Lucille', rather than 'Four hundred'

☆

'Israel in 4 BC had no masturbation'

'Israel in 4 BC had no mass communication'
(*Jesus Christ, Superstar*)

Mistaken Identity

Like a bridge over trouble, Walter

The trouble with Walter is that he doesn't exist, or not in Simon and Garfunkel's 'Bridge Over Troubled Water', anyway.

Further cases of mistaken identity

'We are ancient Sophocles'

A mishearing of the words 'We are agents of the free' in REM's 'Orange Crush'

'You and me and Leslie'

A mondegreen of 'You and me endlessly' from 'Groovin'' by The Young Rascals

'Partially saved was Mary and Tom'

Alternative words for 'Parsley, sage, rosemary and thyme' in 'Scarborough Fair'

'Did Parsley save Rosemary in time?'

Question asked by a young child after hearing
the Simon and Garfunkel lyrics

☆

'Clown Control to Mao Tse-tung'

A mishearing of 'Ground control to Major Tom'
in David Bowie's 'Space Oddity'

☆

'I can see clearly now Lorraine has gone'

Jimmy Cliff preferred to sing that he could see clearly
because 'the rain is gone' in 'I Can See Clearly Now'

☆

*'I wanna know
Have you ever seen Lorraine?'*

Creedence Clearwater Revival hadn't seen Lorraine,
but they had seen 'the rain'

☆

'You called me a tramp'

A paranoid mishearing of 'We're caught in a trap'
from 'Suspicious Minds' by Elvis Presley

☆

'Strawberry Fields For Trevor'

The Beatles preferred to sing 'Strawberry fields for ever'

'Hey Jew'

An unfortunate mishearing of 'Hey Jude'
by The Beatles

'Wave to Dave and wave to Mike'

A mishearing of Freddie Fender's song,
'Wasted Days and Wasted Nights'

'You used to say "Eddy, you loved me"'

Katrina and the Waves favoured 'Baby, you loved me'
from 'I'm Walking on Sunshine'

'He's a vile stoned cowboy'

A slanderous interpretation of Kenny Rogers's
'Rhinestone Cowboy'

'Sue Lawley'

A famous mondegreen of 'So Lonely' by The Police

'Don't cry for me, I'm the cleaner'

A mishearing of 'Don't cry for me, Argentina'
from the musical *Evita*

'Hold me closer, Tony Danza'

The correct lyric, 'Hold me closer, tiny dancer',
comes from Elton John's 'Tiny Dancer'

'A chance to find a Felix on the flame'

Duran Duran were actually referring to 'a phoenix on the
flame' in 'A View to a Kill'

'Sweet Jesus is Thy Name'

A mishearing of 'Sweet dreams are made of this'
by Eurythmics

I'm a Roman

Brian goes before Pontius Pilate, who has a problem
pronouncing his Rs:

BRIAN: 'I am not Jewish, I'm a Roman.'
PONTIUS PILATE [incredulous]: 'A Woman?!'
BRIAN: 'No no, Roman.' [Guard strikes him.] 'Agh!'
PONTIUS PILATE: 'So, your father was a Woman?
Who was he?'

Extract from the 1979 film
Monty Python's Life of Brian

Your name doesn't ring true

A Mr Goldring claims that his family acquired its name through a mishearing. When his grandfather arrived in Britain as an immigrant, confusion occurred over the questions 'What is your name?' and 'Do you have anything to declare?' All he declared was a gold ring . . .

Did anyone see my dog – all four, that is?

At the outset of his career, the Norwegian anthropologist, writer and explorer Thor Heyerdahl (author of *Kon-Tiki* etc.) was interviewed by the BBC. Afterwards, the corporation duly arranged for a taxi to take him home. He waited anxiously outside the entrance, but although taxis came and went, his name was not called. Spotting a cab idling close by, he went over and asked the driver if he was there to collect him. 'Not me, mate,' the cabbie replied. 'I'm here to collect four Airedales.'

> **'Something in the windows learned my name . . .'**
>
> A mishearing of 'Something in the wind has learned my name' from the Carpenters' song 'Top of the World'

It's a little more than loss of hearing, I'm afraid

When Valdemar Lopes de Moraes, a Brazilian farmer and father of two, found himself suffering from ear trouble and muffled hearing, he paid a visit to his local clinic in the town of Montes Claros. When he heard his name called out in the waiting room, he promptly went into a consulting room – where a doctor was performing vasectomies.

'The strangest thing is that he asked no questions when the doctor started preparations in the area which had so little to do with his ear,' said clinic manager Vanessa Guimaraes.

In fact, Mr de Moraes later told staff he thought his ear infection had spread to his testicles.

In Mr de Moraes's defence, the true vasectomy patient was called 'Aldemar', which does sound very like 'Valdemar'. Nevertheless, clinic staff were adamant that they called out the man's full name: Aldemar Aparecido Rodrigues.

Rain Man

The 1988 film *Rain Man*, starring Tom Cruise and Dustin Hoffman, hinges on the mishearing of the name 'Raymond'.

On the death of his father, a materialistic car salesman (Charlie Babbitt) expects to inherit a fortune, but all he receives is a car, while his autistic older brother Raymond inherits all his father's money. At first Charlie is furious, as he didn't know he had a brother, and he tries to swindle

Raymond by seeking to gain custody of him, all the while infuriated by his brother's autistic behaviour. As the two of them bond, however, not only does Raymond's remarkable memory win them a gambling fortune, but Charlie eventually realizes that the person he called 'Rain Man', who used to sing him to sleep when he was a baby, was his forgotten older brother Raymond.

Suits you, Sir

In Shakira's 'Underneath Your Clothes', she sings 'There's the man I chose. There's my territory' rather than 'There's the man I chose. There's my Teletubby.'

TED STRIKER: 'Surely you can't be serious?'
DR RUMACK: 'I am serious, and don't call me Shirley!'

From the US comedy film *Airplane*

The Birds and the Bees

The name's Bond . . .

A woman decided that her son and daughter ought to call their private parts by their proper names. However, she was a little taken back when her son said: 'Penis? Oh, like Penis Brosnan, you mean?'

Venus (fly) trap

A policeman confessed to this one: 'You know that lyric "I'm your Venus" by Bananarama? Well, as a kid I used to sing, "I'm your penis". I wasn't trying to be funny, I'd just never heard of "a Venus".'

'Emily and Ivory'

A mishearing of the Paul McCartney/Stevie Wonder hit 'Ebony and Ivory'

Cheesed off with the G spot

A lady in Kent revealed that her husband, who admittedly has some trouble with his hearing, was suffering under a rather strange misapprehension. Whenever he overheard people talking about the 'G spot', he heard the word 'cheeseboard'. Obviously, this led to a bit of confusion. 'I'm happy to say that I've now set him straight on this matter,' the wife confided – several bries and camemberts later.

Answers teachers received during sex-education lessons

'When a man mates with a woman
he puts his peanuts into her'

'Eggs are made in the ovens'

'Sperm is made in a sack of balls'

A Case of Dirty-Mindedness?

The following examples are all proof that what is at the forefront of our mind affects the way our brain processes what we hear.

☆

'Thrust in me when I say'

A mishearing of 'Trust in me when I say' from 'You're Just Too Good to be True' sung by the Supremes

Builder's brain

After a recent meeting with a builder, a woman was getting into her car when she exclaimed out loud, 'Ouch, my arm hurts,' to which the builder responded, 'What's wrong with your arse?'

'Arm,' she corrected.

'Oh, I thought you said something else,' he muttered, looking embarrassed.

Incensed nether regions

On first hearing, it sounds like the subject of Rick James's 'Super Freak' has 'incense in her genitals', when in fact she has 'incense, wine and candles'.

'Excuse me?'

One of the most often quoted mondegreens is ''Scuse me while I kiss this guy,' which originates from 'Excuse me while I kiss the sky' from the song 'Purple Haze' by Jimi Hendrix. Aware of the mishearing, Hendrix sometimes played up to it – occasionally kissing a guy after performing the line.

Put some clothes on, will you?

''Cause it doesn't make a difference
If we're naked or not'

Well, it does make a difference when the correct words to Bon Jovi's 'Livin' on a Prayer' have nothing to do with nudity, as the correct lyric ends simply 'If we make it or not.'

You may have boobed . . .

According to *The Los Angeles Times*, when a Spanish-style restaurant serving tapas opened in downtown Long Beach, officials were worried that people would mishear 'tapas bar' as 'topless bar'.

X-tra curricular activities

A former Norwich schoolboy recalled how his house-master would often make the following announcement in the refectory: '"The debating society will be gathering together this lunchtime for a *mass debate*. All newcomers welcome to come along." Of course, we schoolboys would hoot with laughter. To this day, I don't think he realized why, although the last laugh could have been on us.'

Dirty rotten slip-ups: a medley

MONDEGREEN: *'Climb every woman'*
CORRECT LYRIC: 'I'm every woman'
(Chaka Khan, 'I'm Every Woman')

MONDEGREEN: *'I got my first real sex dream,
I was five at the time'*
CORRECT LYRIC: 'I got my first real six-string,
Bought it at the five-and-dime'
(Bryan Adams, 'Summer of '69')

☆

MONDEGREEN: *'They reach into your room, whoa
To feel your genitals'*
CORRECT LYRIC: '. . . Just feel their gentle touch'
(Elton John, 'Sad Songs Say So Much')

☆

MONDEGREEN: *'Take your pants down
and make it happen'*
CORRECT LYRIC: 'Take your passion . . .'
(Irene Cara, 'What a Feeling')

☆

MONDEGREEN: *'Bill Oddie, Bill Oddie,
put your hands all over my body'*
CORRECT LYRIC: 'Erotic, erotic . . .'
(Madonna, 'Erotic')

☆

MONDEGREEN: *'I'm cold and I'm in chains,
Bound and broken on the floor'*
CORRECT LYRIC: 'I'm cold and I'm ashamed . . .'
(Natalie Imbruglia, 'Torn')

MONDEGREEN: *'Only the lonely get laid'*
CORRECT LYRIC: 'Only the lonely can play'
(The Motels, 'Only the Lonely')

☆

MONDEGREEN: *'Chop the gooly near his knees'*
CORRECT LYRIC: 'Tropical the island breeze'
(Madonna, 'La Isla Bonita')

☆

MONDEGREEN: *'Are you straight or bi?'*
CORRECT LYRIC: 'Leave your cares behind'
(Chic, 'Good Times')

☆

MONDEGREEN: *'I'm going naked to Heaven'*
CORRECT LYRIC: 'I'm gonna make it to Heaven'
(Irene Cara, 'Fame')

☆

MONDEGREEN: *'I can't get it up'*
CORRECT LYRIC: 'I cannot give it up'
(Robbie Williams, 'Feel')

The Dating Game

It's a game

When Player sang 'You can blame it all on me' from 'Baby Come Back', some heard 'You can play Monopoly.'

I've got some news for you . . .

During an episode of the satirical BBC news quiz *Have I Got News For You*, guest-hosted by actress Joan Collins, the following exchange took place:

MICHAEL WINNER: 'French farmers are celebrated.'
JOAN COLLINS: 'Celibate? No wonder the population of France is so low.'

> ### *'All my lovers, I will send to you'*
>
> A mishearing of The Beatles' lyric 'All my loving,
> I will send to you'

Just call me

In the 1968 song 'Angel of the Morning' by Merrilee Rush
and the Turnabouts, some listeners have erroneously heard
'Just brush your teeth before you leave me, baby' instead
of 'Just touch my cheek . . .'

It's a gamble

'I see a pair of dice' is a mishearing of 'I see a paradise'
from 'Nothing's Gonna Stop Us Now' by Starship.

Wedding Gaffes and Funeral Blues

WEDDING GUESTS often complain that they cannot hear the speeches, especially if they are at the back of the room, or the speakers are speaking too fast or too quietly, or the microphone is playing up, and invariably certain words can get lost or misunderstood, with amusing consequences.

'To the bride and groom'

I once attended a wedding where the bride was English and the groom from India. The couple had done their best to include traditions from both cultures and all was going well until the best man, himself from India, started his speech.

In a loud, but heavily accented voice he began, 'Fornication . . .' There was a long pause from the best man, a disbelieving silence from his audience, then he coughed and tried again: 'For an occasion such as today . . .'

Of course, he did this deliberately, but at first none of us could believe our ears, and to this day I'm not sure that everyone understood it was a joke.

'A jest's prosperity lies in the ear
Of him that hears it, never in the tongue
Of him that makes it.'

WILLIAM SHAKESPEARE, *Love's Labour's Lost*

The wedding breakfast

A friend told me that she once went to a Catholic wedding near Stratford-upon-Avon. It was a beautiful day, the bride looked stunning, and the village church was suitably quaint. However, the service went on and on and on. As the vicar was doing his spiel on the Lamb of God, my friend could have sworn the chap behind her said, 'May thee come with mint sauce.'

Thinking that she had found a kindred spirit, she turned and responded with 'May the peas of the Lord go with it.' Unfortunately, the man maintained his stony-faced demeanour, leaving her to wonder if she had heard what she thought she'd heard, or whether she should have eaten breakfast before setting out.

'Someone Shaved My Wife Tonight'

A mishearing of Elton John's 1975 song
'Someone Saved My Life Tonight'

Something a bit woolly

At a recent spring wedding the bride, who had a great fondness for sheep, chose to be attended by a lamb. Once the service was concluded, the lamb went off to decorate the area where champagne was being served. A latecomer, spotting the animal, turned to the groom's brother and asked him who was the fellow who was looking after the lamb. Glancing over at the man in wellies and a Barbour, the groom's brother replied, 'Oh, that's the farmer . . .'

The guest, however, heard this as 'Oh, that's the father . . .' and for the rest of the day remained baffled at the father of the bride's seemingly bizarre choice of wedding attire.

'You can dance, you can die, having the time of your life'

A popular mishearing of Abba's 'You can dance, you can jive . . .' from 'Dancing Queen'

That was her funeral?

At the start of my great-aunt Catherine's funeral, which I attended with her niece (my aunt), the vicar began by explaining that we were gathered to pay our last respects to '. . . oh, I can't quite read this, is it Catherine . . . ?'

'Diment,' a relative quickly filled in (as in die-ment).

'Yes, Catherine Dement,' said the vicar (as in demented).

'Diment,' urged the relative.

'Dement,' said the vicar.

At this point my aunt and I simultaneously became subject to a fit of the giggles. In fact we had to pretend that we were crying. I was very fond of my great-aunt, but I do hope she wasn't looking down at that moment.

Anyone know where the Holy Ghost went?

When Luela Palmer attended a funeral, the words she heard as the coffin was lowered into the ground were: 'Glory be to the Father, and to the Son, into the hole he goes . . .'

'There's a bin full of ashes on the forty-five'

A mishearing of the first line from 'Brimful of Asha' by Cornershop

---

Up the Garden Path

A case of being left red in the neck

It was a scorching day, and a City chap, at his weekend cottage in the country, had given up trying to dig up the baked earth to create a rose garden. He was very grateful, therefore, when his competent, strapping neighbour took over. After some half-hour of spadework, the neighbour was most gratified when the City chap's wife came up to him and said, 'Did you know you're an expert?' So he redoubled his efforts, toiling through the heat.

That evening, job finally done, the men were sitting having a beer. The neighbour rubbed the back of his neck and remarked that it was really very sore.

'Well, I did warn you,' said the lady of the house.

'You did?' he replied.

'Yes, when I came out into the garden earlier, I said to you, "Did you know your neck's burnt!"'

Andy walks with me

A popular mondegreen involves a child being asked what God's first name is, to which he confidently replies, 'Andy'. This name derives from the hymn 'In the Garden', which features the telling words, 'And he [Andy] walks with me, And he [Andy] talks with me, And he [Andy] tells me I am his own . . .'

Military and Political Blunders

The Light Brigade makes heavy work of it

'Haffely, Gaffely, Gaffely, Gonward.' No wonder the Light Brigade found itself in a muddle! Someone had indeed blundered.

> 'Half a league, half a league,
> Half a league onward,
> All in the valley of Death
> Rode the six hundred.'

'Haffely, Gaffely . . .' is a modern mishearing of Tennyson's famous poem about the British Light Cavalry Brigade's heroic, but misguided, charge against Russian forces during the Crimean War. (The reason for the mishearing becomes clearer if you say the words in an American accent.)

'Crimea River'

A mishearing of 'Cry Me a River' by Julie London

Well, we'll need a few farmhands

In 2001, a *Times* reader wrote to the newspaper to tell the story of her father's registration for potential call-up at the outbreak of the Second World War. When asked what he did for a living he replied 'pharmacist', but instead the clerk wrote down 'farm assistant'.

You'll make it . . .

During the Second World War, an unconscious American Army Air Force major was brought to an Australian hospital in Port Moresby, New Guinea. Slowly waking up the next day, he asked the nursing sister, 'Was I brought here to die?'

'Oh no, sir,' she replied, 'you were brought here yesterday.'

Did you hear the one about that John Brown guy?

The subject of the American Civil War song 'John Brown's Body' is generally assumed to be the famed American abolitionist, while others believe John Brown was a Scotsman who was a member of the 12th Massachusetts Regiment.

One anonymous person admits to having been a little confused about the first line of the song: 'John Brown's body lies a-mouldering in the grave.' For quite some time he was under the mistaken impression that the corpse lay 'moulting' in the grave.

The true words keep marching on

'The Battle Hymn of the Republic' was written by Julia Ward Howe in December 1861, after the outbreak of the American Civil War. The actual words begin:

*'Mine eyes have seen the glory of the coming of the Lord:
He is trampling out the vintage where the grapes
of wrath are stored.'*

However, one little girl got confused about the American wildlife. According to her version: 'He is trampling on the village where the great giraffe is stored.'

Do your ears hear?

In the traditional (but bizarre) children's song 'Do Your Ears Hang Low?', the line 'Can you throw 'em over your shoulder / Like a Continental soldier?' has produced a couple of interesting mishearings. One individual with some strange ideas of soldiering heard the lyric as 'cotton-pickin' soldier', while another thought it was 'cotton ninja soldier'.

OK, we get the message

Wireless messages and signals are famous for causing confusion, as these examples demonstrate . . .

'Send three-and-fourpence, we're going to a dance'

('Send reinforcements. We're going to advance'
– First World War)

'Keep off the virgins: they're mine'

('Keep off the verges; they're mined' – Second World War)

'Rommel captured. Send assistance'

(Camel ruptured. Send assistance' – a signal reputedly
sent by a British officer on an undercover mission behind
enemy lines in the Western Desert, Second World War)

'Good dads are going to fight the bad dads'

A child's explanation for the US bombing of Baghdad,
as published in Canadian newspaper, *The Globe and Mail*

The Gulf between hearing and meaning

The following conversation took place recently in a Kent classroom:

YOUNG BOY (in Reception class): 'My Daddy's off to the golf.'

TEACHER (adopting sombre tone): 'Oh, that must be hard for you and your Mummy. Do you know how long your Daddy will be away for?'

YOUNG BOY: 'Oh, just the weekend. I'm going to play too when I'm big.'

Mass debaters

A listener caught the end of a BBC radio discussion programme with Harriet Harman, and could have sworn he heard her say 'Masturbate immediately!' He only later discovered that her actual words were: 'This is an issue the Labour Party must debate immediately.'

'Apartheid Lover'

A mishearing of Stevie Wonder's
'Part-Time Lover'

TV, Film and Stage

'Goodbye, Missed the Chips'

The above should of course, be *Goodbye, Mr Chips*, after the title character in a 1934 novel by James Hilton (and later a Hollywood film) about an ageing English school-master – Charles 'Chips' Chipping.

In his 1974 autobiography *My Word*, Frank Muir went one better when he cleverly misquoted the original book title as 'Good pie, missed the chips.'

The actual words just happen to be . . .

The Sound of Music is one of the most successful movies in all cinema history. Love it or loathe it, few of us can fail to be familiar with 'Do-Re-Mi' and 'Edelweiss' – can we?

On the subject of Maria, the film's main character, these two older nuns discuss her unusual merits:

AGATHA: 'She's always late for chapel'
SOPHIA: 'But her *ten pence worth* is real' (penitence)

Or perhaps 'her *pantyhose* is real'?

Rather than being 'an asset to' the abbey, poor Maria has been assumed, by some, to be more like 'an abscess in' the abbey.

Meanwhile, Captain von Trapp's eldest daughter Liesl revealed that she was timid, shy and scared 'of things beyond my ken'. One little girl in a pale pink coat misheard this line, however, and it took her many years to work out who 'Ken' was (or rather, wasn't) in the story.

Could these really be Maria's favourite things?

'And *nits fried* with noodles'
('schnitzel . . .')

'Tea, a drink with *German* bread'
('. . . jam and bread')

And is this the song Captain von Trapp wished to sing with his family?

'*Idle vice, idle vice*,
bless my homeland for ever'
('Edelweiss')

What about his children's goodbye to his party guests?

'So long, farewell
Oh, what are we to say?'
(. . . Au revoir, auf Wiedersehen)

Finally, Maria should take inspiration from these words:

'Climb every mountain
Fall in every stream' (ford)

Unenchanted evening

'*Sam and Janet evening*
You may see a strangler'

'*You'll see the Lone Ranger*
Across a crowded room'

The above lines are mishearings that afflicted Oscar Hammerstein's original lyrics for 'Some Enchanted Evening' from the musical *South Pacific,* in which 'you may see a stranger' across a crowded room.

'*How do you solve a problem like diarrhoea?*'

A complaint about Andrew Lloyd Webber's method of picking his new Maria von Trapp using a Saturday-night television programme, *How Do You Solve a Problem Like Maria?*, which involved the audience voting at the end

Ding dong . . .

'Somewhere over the rainbow, weigh a pie'

Obviously Dorothy Gale was not off to cook dinner in Oz. The land that she dreamed of over the rainbow was 'way up high'.

A fan of *The Wizard of Oz*, which starred Judy Garland, found her sibling's reaction to the film somewhat off-putting: 'My sister used to sing "Ding Dong! The Witch is dead. Which old Witch? The silly bitch!" [instead of 'the wicked Witch']. She was quite small, so I think she must have thought those were the words. Unfortunately, those are the ones I always hear now.'

No 'Memory' for the words, or just a mishearing?

'Archie. It's so easy to leave me'

'Every street lamp seems to beat a fatal lipstick warning'

In 'Memory', from Andrew Lloyd Webber's musical *Cats*, Grizabella the Glamour Cat actually sings 'Touch me' rather than 'Archie', and the street lamps beat a 'fatalistic warning'.

My face lady . . .

In Lerner and Loewe's musical *My Fair Lady*, did Henry Higgins ever let slip the words, 'I've thrown a custard in her face' instead of 'I've grown accustomed to her face'? And maybe some listeners assumed he was thinking about Eliza's extravagant new outfits when they heard him sing 'I've sewn a costume to her face.'

Summertime, and the lyrics ain't easy

'Summertime' is an aria composed by George Gershwin for his 1935 opera *Porgy and Bess*. The original lyrics are by DuBose Heyward and Ira Gershwin, unlike the following line:

> *'Suppertime, and the liver is greasy'*
> ('Summertime, and the living is easy')

Bring on the smelling salts . . .

In the Richard Rodgers and Oscar Hammerstein musical *Carousel*, the song 'You'll Never Walk Alone' is sung after the death of Billy Bigelow, to give courage to his daughter.

Sadly, 'You'll Never Wear Cologne' lacks the rousing spirit that lifted the hearts of the show's original wartime audiences, and later those of many British football fans (particularly Liverpool supporters).

Wandering away from the original

'I was born, and I'm a-wandrin' far' is one unique interpretation of the song 'I Was Born Under a Wanderin' Star' from the musical *Paint Your Wagon*.

Grease is the word

The title song from the musical *Grease* may be the word, but not when it's sung as 'Three cents a word.'

These devoted fans were also somewhat hopeless with the words of the song 'Hopelessly Devoted To You':

'Hope this lady voted for you'

'Hope I eat a doughnut with you'

'Hope the city voted for you'

Lastly, what can one say of the fan who belted out 'Grease is the worst' – perhaps she wasn't a fan after all?

You could cry, or was that buy?

A fan of the musical *Evita* obviously had a little trouble grasping its premise. In her version, Argentina's most famous first lady sings the words, 'Don't cry for me, Marge and Tina' – a couple of *descamisados*, perhaps.

Knocking Eva Perón off her pedestal a bit further, during a rendition of the song 'High Flying Adored', a young man in the audience was sure he heard Che Guevara ask Eva whether she believed she'd become the lady of 'the mall'. Eva's shopping habits aside, the last two words should have been 'them all'.

Incidentally, David Essex, who played Che Guevara in the original production, did not have a number-two hit in the charts with 'A Winter Sale', but rather 'A Winter's Tale'.

Ok-lahoma

On a recent episode of the BBC chat show *Friday Night with Jonathan Ross*, two of the guests included Andrew Lloyd Webber and John Barrowman, who were promoting their Saturday-night television show *Any Dream Will Do*. Wrapping up the interview, Ross asked them to name their best musical of all time. While Lloyd Webber said *West Side Story*, Barrowman revealed that his was *Oklahoma*. He then told of an occasion when, during a performance of the eponymous song, the cast pulled a prank on their audience.

Instead of singing the word 'Ok-lahoma' (there is a long pause after the 'Ok-'), the cast sang 'I'm [pause] a homo'. He did not say if anyone in the audience reported a mishearing.

There's a bone to pick with this one

In the 1957 musical play *The Music Man*, 'Seventy-Six Trombones' ('Seventy-six trombones led the big parade . . .') is the signature song that 'Professor' Harold Hill uses to encourage the townspeople of 'River City' to imagine their children playing in an enormous marching band.

In 2004, a *Los Angeles Times* reader told how the song had inspired her seven-year-old son to sing 'Seventy-six strong bones led the big parade.'

Four candles

One of the best-loved comic moments on British television is *The Two Ronnies* sketch 'The Hardware Shop', more commonly known as 'Four Candles'. In it, Ronnie Corbett is working behind the counter in a hardware shop, while Ronnie Barker is the customer. A number of deliberate mishearings crop up in the scene, including 'four candles' for 'fork handles' ('handles for forks') and 'sore tips' for 'saw tips' ('tips for covering saws').

Doctor Who?

'I am a garlic, I will exterminate,' chanted five-year-old William Jones after an episode of *Doctor Who*. An avid fan of the programme, he regularly discusses the properties of 'Garlics' with his peers. Despite being corrected on several occasions, Garlics remain his arch-enemy of choice.

☆

On the subject of *Doctor Who*, in the 2007 episode 'Human Nature', the Doctor found himself in the middle of a love scene and uttered the words to his romantic interest: 'You are far too beautiful . . .' My five-year-old son, who had been glued to the screen – scary scarecrows and all – thereupon asked, 'Why is she farting beautifully?'

LIGHTNING McQUEEN: 'He won three Piston Cups!'
MATER: 'He did what in his cup!?'

From the movie Cars

All That Jazz
and Other Folk

Jazzing up the conversation

A lady arranging a family day out with another family suggested a visit to a local castle where a jousting tournament was to take place. 'Oh, my husband loves jazz. Let's go there,' said the other wife. The first lady repeated 'jousting'; the second replied, 'Jazz sing-along, great!' The first lady, wondering if her friend had ever heard of knights in shining armour, gave up, and left the smaller details to her friend's eyes rather than her ears.

> ### 'I've Got You Under My Sink'
>
> A mishearing of 'I've Got You Under My Skin', a popular Cole Porter song

Elephant ears

Ever heard of the famous jazz singer 'Elephants Gerald', otherwise known as Ella Fitzgerald?

Taking the rap

A young girl thought that George Gershwin's *Rhapsody in Blue* was 'Rap City in Blue'.

The rest is . . . ?

The jazz musician Steve Swallow reportedly said about jazz composition, 'Eventually, an idea always comes, and then the rest is science.' Had he used the original quotation correctly however, the rest would have been 'silence'. ('The rest is silence' – *Hamlet*, William Shakespeare)

Back to chapter one

In the 1947 film *The Shocking Miss Pilgrim* (music by George Gershwin and lyrics by Ira Gershwin and Kay Swift), there is a song called 'Aren't You Kind Of Glad We Did?' In the middle verse the actual words are 'On my good name there will be doubt cast / With never a sign of any chaperone.' The famous jazz singer Sarah Vaughan, however, sang the last line as 'With never a sign of any chapter one.'

Oh, Susanna

'I've come from Alabama with a Band-Aid on my knee' is a mishearing of this popular folk song, which substitutes the word 'banjo' with a brand of sticking plaster.

'Chuck me a lady tonight'

'Luck be a lady tonight' is the correct lyric
in the song 'Luck Be a Lady' from the musical
Guys and Dolls

Oh, my darling

According to some misguided listeners, the fate of Clementine (the subject of Percy Montrose's famous song) hinged on some misplaced chewie: 'You have lost *your gum* for ever / Dreadful sorry, Clementine' when in truth the poor woman was 'lost and gone for ever . . .'

Did you hear the one sung by the Irishman?

From *The Corkman* came a tale of one man's unique interpretation of Frank Sinatra's classic 'Strangers in the Night'. This particular chap obviously wasn't too taken with the original opening lines – 'Strangers in the night, exchanging glances, wondering in the night . . .' – and had come up with his own slightly more violent version: 'Strangers have a knife, exchanging glasses, wandering with the knife . . .'

---

*'I'm wild again, defiled again,
a simple and wittering child again'*

An unfortunate mishearing of 'I'm wild again, beguiled again, a simpering, whimpering child again' from 'Bewitched, Bothered and Bewildered'

Jolly good

'For he's a jolly good fellow that nobody can *divide*' (deny)

Dancing to the wrong tune

In 2001, a *Times* reader wrote to the paper to tell of a mondegreen that she recalled from her youth. As she and her friends learned a folk dance together while listening to the tune 'A Merry Conceit', her father asked someone to confirm the name of the music, only to be unreliably informed that the song was called 'American Seat'.

You've Taken a Wrong Turn

The following are examples of mondegreens involving places and place names.

'Wouldn't it be good to be in Yorkshire?'

A mishearing of Nik Kershaw's 'Wouldn't It Be Good (To Be In Your Shoes)?'

'Wait in Rome as the music starts'

A mishearing of the lyric 'Swaying room as the music starts' from Madonna's 'Crazy For You'

'Stop in the Neighbourhood'

A mishearing of the song 'Stop in the Name of Love' by Diana Ross and The Supremes

☆

'She's got a ticket to Rye'

A mishearing of The Beatles' 'She's Got A Ticket To Ride'

'I need a Plaistow hideaway'

A mishearing of the lyric 'I need a place to hide away'
from 'Yesterday' by The Beatles

'People will say we're in Hove'

A mishearing of 'People will say we're in love' from the
musical *Oklahoma*

Bathroom Habits

> ### *'I sauntered north and flossed my teeth'*
>
> 'I saw a northbound flock of geese . . .'
> were Johnny Cash's actual lyrics in the song
> 'Flesh and Blood'

Rock bottom

'Last Night A Bidet Saved My Life' – this seems an unlikely scenario, and so it is, for the correct song title is 'Last Night A DJ Saved My Life . . .' by Indeep.

> ### *'All you did was wet my bed'*
>
> A mishearing of 'All you did was wreck my bed'
> from Rod Stewart's 'Maggie May'

Where are the gents?

'There's a bathroom on the right' is a famous mondegreen of 'There's a bad moon on the rise' from Creedence Clearwater Revival's 'Bad Moon Rising'.

Diamond-encrusted lavatories

Whenever a friend heard the song 'Lucy in the Sky with Diamonds', she always imagined that The Beatles were singing 'Loo Seat in the Sky with Diamonds'. She knew they couldn't be the real words, but once heard, never forgotten.

Troublesome toilets

It has been said that children studying *Macbeth* often say 'double double, toilet trouble' instead of 'double double, toil and trouble'. However, many adults don't get it right either, favouring 'Bubble bubble, toil and trouble.'

Beware of floating fridges

Simon and Garfunkel's 'Bridge Over Troubled Water' lyrics are the subject of yet more mishearings with 'Like a bridge o'er a tub of water, I won't let you drown,' and 'Like a fridge dropped in troubled water.'

Trouble with the Queen's English

I swear that is not what you heard Her Majesty say

When The Kinks singer Ray Davies went to pick up his CBE at Buckingham Palace in 2004, a couple of months after being shot by a mugger in New Orleans, he was surprised to hear of the Queen's concern for his health.

Davies claimed he had heard Her Majesty say 'I hope they catch the bastards who shot you!' though officials at the Palace deemed this to be a mishearing.

> **'Uptown girl, she's been living in her white-trade world'**
>
> A mishearing of the lyric 'white-bread world' in the song 'Uptown Girl' by Billy Joel

To serve the King

Perhaps more of a misunderstanding than a mondegreen, when King Henry II uttered the words 'Will no one rid me of this turbulent priest?' most historians are agreed that he did not desire the murder of the Archbishop of Canterbury. It was, therefore, a catastrophic misinterpretation by the four knights Reginald Fitzurse, Hugh de Moreville, William de Traci and Richard Brito, which, on 29 December 1170, resulted in the murder of Thomas à Becket inside Canterbury Cathedral.

'I know that you believe that you understood what you think I said, but I am not sure you realize that what you heard is not what I meant.'

Robert McCloskey,
State Department spokesman
(attributed)

Regardez les citrons

A Londoner on holiday in France was enjoying a conversation with his walking guide, who spoke very good English. All was going well, until the Englishman mentioned that he very much liked Citroëns. 'Lemons?' the Frenchman asked, seeming somewhat puzzled that the conversation had moved on to food. Surprisingly, it took a good few minutes for it to become clear that the Englishman had been referring to cars, not *citrons*.

Accentuate the positive

In 2001, a *Times* reader related the tale of how a Scottish friend of his mother once happened to mention that the Countess of Ayr was coming for tea the following day. However, the visitor (rather disappointingly) turned out to be the 'county surveyor'.

In another letter to *The Times,* a former employee in the Foreign and Commonwealth Office, Sarah Rowland Jones, described the time when she took a call from someone who presumably assumed that the Diplomatic Service was only staffed by 'aristocratic or highly decorated gentlemen', because he asked if he could speak to Sir Rowland Jones.

'He is the very pine-apple of politeness!'

MRS MALAPROP, a character from *The Rivals*, by Richard Brinsley Sheridan

Work on those aitches . . .

Last summer a friend was with a group of children who were taught the following rhyme by an entertainer:

I one my teacher
I two my teacher

I three my teacher
I four my teacher
I five my teacher
I six my teacher
I seven my teacher
I eight my teacher

They thought it was hilarious, but she was interested to learn that half of them thought they had eaten their teacher, and the other that they hated said teacher.

An American in London

An American lady called a London radio show and told the presenter (Sarah Kennedy) that her husband had asked 'What's with this Chelsea Flasher?' He meant the Chelsea Flower Show – try it out for size with an American accent.

'Take care of the sense, and the sounds will take care of themselves.'

Alice in Wonderland
LEWIS CARROLL

How Sound Will Travel

One small mishearing . . .

'That's one small step for man, one giant leap for mankind'

We have all heard Neil Armstrong's famous, if apparently contradictory, words as he left the *Apollo 11* space lander and became the first man to set foot on the moon. Afterwards, however, Armstrong insisted that he thought he had said, and indeed meant to say, 'one small step for *a* man'. Those back on earth, though, heard otherwise, and even Neil Armstrong couldn't be sure.

In 2006, Australian computer expert Peter Shann Ford ran the NASA recording through sound-editing software and clearly picked up an acoustic wave from the word 'a'. Evidently, Armstrong spoke the word at a rate of 35 milli-seconds, which is ten times too fast for it to be audible. Officials at Nasa have since met Mr Ford to discuss his findings, and have instructed their own analysts to run in-house tests.

1ST ELDERLY WOMAN ON BUS: Is this Wembley?
2ND DITTO: No, it's Thursday.
3RD DITTO: Yes, I am too.

Cut that ...

'Rocket man, burning up the trees on every lawn'

A mishearing of 'Rocket man, burning out his fuse up here alone' from 'Rocket Man' by Elton John

And you come to me ...

'And you come to me on a submarine'

A mishearing of 'And you come to me on a summer breeze' from The Bee Gees' 'How Deep Is Your Love?'

It's plain enough

'Daniel is driving tonight on a plane'

A common mishearing of the line 'Daniel is travelling tonight on a plane' written by Bernie Taupin and sung by Elton John

> *'Trying hard to control my car'*
>
> A mishearing of the line 'Trying hard to control my heart', in Madonna's 'Crazy For You'

Car trouble

A reader wrote to *The San Francisco Chronicle* to tell of an occasion, some years before, when her family had been driving through the mountains of North Carolina. They had come to a sign announcing that they had arrived at Carroll Gap, and, as the view was spectacular, her father suggested that they stop to look at it. However, her sister had heard 'Car-roll Gap', and became extremely frightened that their car was about to career down the steep mountainside.

> *'I wanted to be the mother of your Toyota Now it's just farewell'*
>
> An unlikely mishearing of the lines 'I wanted to be the mother of your child, And now it's just farewell' in the song 'I Can't Be With You' by The Cranberries

Wrong road

'We built this city on the wrong damn road'

A mishearing of 'We built this city on rock 'n' roll'
in Starship's 'We Built This City'

'A depraved pair of guys
Put up a parking lot'

'A pink pair of dice
Put in a parking lot'

The correct version from Joni Mitchell's
'Big Yellow Taxi' is:
'They paved paradise
And put up a parking lot'

I'm outta here

'Gotta leave you all behind and take a cruise'

In 'Bohemian Rhapsody' by Queen, what Freddie Mercury
was actually suggesting they did was to 'face the truth'.

An A–Z
of Pop Howlers

━━━━━

THERE ARE literally thousands of mondegreens involving the lyrics of pop songs. Many of these – possibly the genuine ones – are gibberish, while some of wittier offerings perhaps make better sense than the original lyrics. Certainly, at one time or another, most of us have been caught belting out the wrong words to a pop song. Perhaps we didn't listen hard enough to the words, or maybe the poor diction of the vocalists was at fault, or the words themselves didn't make any sense in the first place, so we made up new ones instead. For some, the consequences have been embarrassing. So next time you find yourself at the karaoke machine, do read the words.

(A–Z by Artist)

A

HOWLER: 'Mum, it's me here, here you go again'
ORIGINAL: 'Mamma Mia, here I go again'
            (Abba, 'Mamma Mia')

B

HOWLER: 'Save all your kippers for tea'
ORIGINAL: 'Save all your kisses for me'
            (Brotherhood of Man, 'Save Your Kisses
            For Me')

C
HOWLER: 'Fame, I'm gonna live for ever
Faintly remember my name'
ORIGINAL: '. . . Baby, remember my name'
(Irene Cara, 'Fame')

D
HOWLER: 'Stand on the line, in disco and rhyme'
ORIGINAL: 'Straddle the line in discord and rhyme'
(Duran Duran, 'Hungry Like the Wolf')

E
HOWLER: 'If I find the end of the rope,
Well, I'll always remember that I had a
swingin' time'
ORIGINAL: 'If I wind up broke up . . .'
(Elvis, 'Viva Las Vegas')

F
HOWLER: 'Texas handyman'
ORIGINAL: 'Textbook hippy man'
(Ben Folds, 'The Ascent of Stan')

G
HOWLER: 'I blow bubbles when you are not here'
ORIGINAL: 'My world crumbles . . .'
(Macy Gray, 'I Try')

H
HOWLER: 'Come Mr Taleban'
ORIGINAL: 'Come Mr Tally Man'
(Harry Belafonte, 'The Banana Boat Song')

I

HOWLER: 'Una pull over blanket'
ORIGINAL: 'Una paloma blanca'
            (Julio Iglesias, 'Paloma Blanca')

J

HOWLER: 'And it seems to me, you've lived your life
            Like a sandal in the bin'
ORIGINAL: '. . . Like a candle in the wind'
            (Elton John, 'Candle in the Wind')

K

HOWLER: 'Telling tales of drunkenness and croquet'
ORIGINAL: 'Telling tales of drunkenness and cruelty'
            (The Kinks, 'Sunny Afternoon')

L

HOWLER: 'Can't stand shaving'
ORIGINAL: 'Constant craving'
            (K. D. Lang, 'Constant Craving')

M

HOWLER: 'Like detergent / Drunk for the very first
            time'
ORIGINAL: 'Like a virgin / Touched for . . .'
            (Madonna, 'Like A Virgin')

N

HOWLER: 'Where, where did my Anadins go?'
ORIGINAL: 'Where, where did my innocence go?'
            (Olivia Newton-John, 'A Little More Love')

O

HOWLER: 'I can eat my dinner in a fancy red sarong'
ORIGINAL: 'I can eat my dinner in a fancy restaurant'
          (Sinead O'Connor, 'Nothing Compares 2 U')

P

HOWLER: 'I'll be watching stew'
ORIGINAL: 'I'll be watching you'
          (The Police, 'Every Breath You Take')

Q

HOWLER: 'Haven't got time to dust'
ORIGINAL: 'Another one bites the dust'
          (Queen, 'Another One Bites the Dust')

R

HOWLER: 'Everybody burps'
ORIGINAL: 'Everybody hurts'
          (REM, 'Everybody Hurts')

S

HOWLER: 'I want your face hair all around me'
ORIGINAL: 'I want your face, yeah, all around me'
          (Savage Garden, 'All Around Me')

T

HOWLER: 'We're living on a pound of eggs and giving off farts'
ORIGINAL: 'We're living in a powder keg and giving off sparks'
          (Bonnie Tyler, 'Total Eclipse of the Heart')

U

HOWLER: 'Someday Buddy Someday'
ORIGINAL: 'Sunday Bloody Sunday'
(U2, 'Sunday Bloody Sunday')

V

HOWLER: 'Why does Mel jump?'
ORIGINAL: 'Might as well jump'
(Van Halen, 'Jump')

W

HOWLER: 'Fart more frequently you're wearing perfume'
ORIGINAL: 'Far more frequently you're wearing perfume'
(Stevie Wonder, 'Lately')

X

HOWLER: 'I am only making plans for night, Jo'
ORIGINAL: 'I am only making plans for Nigel'
(XTC, 'Making Plans For Nigel')

Y

HOWLER: 'Every time you go away, you take a piece of meat with you'
ORIGINAL: 'Every time you go away, you take a piece of me with you'
(Paul Young, 'Every Time You Go Away')

Z

HOWLER: 'Hit me like a tunnel head'
ORIGINAL: 'Hit me like a ton o' lead'
(ZZ Top, 'Gimme All Your Lovin'')

Animal Crackers

SOMETIMES it seems that the animal lovers out there can have a little difficulty assimilating the correct words . . .

'The bright blessed day, the dogs say goodnight'

A mishearing of 'The bright blessed day, the dark sacred night' from 'It's A Wonderful World' by Louis Armstrong

---

A new breed?

In a letter to *The Times* in 2001, a reader from London related how he had been reading the small ads of his local paper when he was puzzled by an advertisement for a 'box of puppies' in the pets column. It dawned on him that it should have been 'boxer puppies'.

'Music has charms to soothe the savage beast'

This is a misquotation from William Congreve's play *The Mourning Bride* (1697). The correct quotation is: 'Musick hath Charms to sooth a savage Breast.'

'*Grim poodle-basher, over forty-five*'

A mondegreen of 'Brimful of Asha on the
forty-five' from Cornershop's 'Brimful of Asha'

A is for aardvark ...

MONDEGREEN:

'*I was born an aardvark*'

ORIGINAL BREED:

'I was born in Li'l Rock'
(Stevie Wonder, 'I Was Made To Love Her')

And armadillo

MONDEGREEN:

'*Everybody needs a good armadillo, everybody needs
a possum*'

ORIGINAL BREED:

'Everyone needs a bosom for pillow, everyone needs
a bosom' (Cornershop, 'Brimful of Asha')

MONDEGREEN:

'Is this the way to armadillo?'

ORIGINAL BREED:

'Is this the way to Amarillo?'
(Tony Christie, '[Is This the Way to] Amarillo?')

(One supposes a slight difference between this Central and South American mammal, sometimes capable of rolling its bony shell into a ball, and sweet Marie's Texan hometown.)

Bird song

Doris K. Ballard thought Patsy Kline was singing 'I Call the Geeses' rather than 'I Fall to Pieces', while another woman has been caught out singing 'I love parrots in the springtime, I love parrots in the fall,' instead of 'I love Paris . . .'

'Like a Bird's Wing'

A mishearing of Madonna's 'Like a Virgin'

Sea life

How about, 'Your walrus hurt the one you love', a mishearing of Connie Francis's 'You Always Hurt the One You Love'?

Or 'Shamu the mysterious whale', a mishearing of the U2 lyric 'She moves in mysterious ways'? Or 'Alex the Seal' (otherwise known as 'Our Lips are Sealed' by The Go-Gos)?

A world of insects

'The ants are my friends, they're blowin' in the wind' is a well-known mishearing of Bob Dylan's words: 'The answer, my friend, is blowin' in the wind.'

Frankie Valli's 1967 song 'Can't Take My Eyes Off (of) You' (also covered by Andy Williams and Engelbert Humperdinck) has spawned the unlikely 'Can't Take My Ants Off (of) You.'

'She's got a tick in her eye'

A mishearing of 'She's got a ticket to ride' by The Beatles

Rodents

'Moon river, why are mice so blue?'

. . . should, of course, be 'Moon river, why am I so blue?'

'Mine is a long, sad tale,' said the Mouse, turning to Alice and sighing deeply.

'It is a long tail, certainly,' said Alice. 'I don't believe I have seen such a long tail.'

'I am not talking about my tail,' said the Mouse, beginning to look offended.

'Please don't take offence!' Alice cried, sitting down close to the Mouse and taking hold of its long tail. 'You haven't even begun to tell us your story, and I'm sure we all want to hear it.'

Alice in Wonderland, LEWIS CARROLL

Amphibians

'The magical mystery toad is coming to take you away'

'The magical mystery tour is coming to take you away'
(The Beatles, 'Magical Mystery Tour')

☆

'Love is a big, fat quivering slug'

More correctly, 'Love is a big, fat river in flood'
from Sting's 'Love is Stronger Than Justice'

Dear deer

'There's a bad moose on the rise'

This well-known mondegreen derives from the lyric 'There's a bad moon on the rise' in Creedence Clearwater Revival's 'Bad Moon Rising'.

'Scary moose, scary moose, will you do the fandango?'

In reality there is no mention of frightening antlered beasts in Queen's hit record 'Bohemian Rhapsody', but rather a reference to Scaramouche, a seventeenth-century Neapolitan actor and also a character from Punch and Judy shows.

'That the twisting kaleidoscope mooses are in turn'

In 'Can You Feel the Love Tonight?' from *The Lion King*, Elton John definitely wasn't singing about 'mooses'. Lyricist Tim Rice's more sensible words were 'The twisting kaleidoscope moves us all in turn.'

'Caribou Queen . . .'

The object of Billy Ocean's affections, 'Caribbean Queen', had two legs rather than four.

> ### 'It's a family of bears'
>
> A mishearing of 'It's a Family Affair' by Sly and the Family Stone

'Heath, cliff, see me, I'm a tree, I'm a wombat.'

With reference to the tragic love between Heathcliff and Catherine Earnshaw in Emily Brontë's novel *Wuthering Heights*, Kate Bush was actually singing 'Heathcliff, it's me, your Cathy, I've come home.'

Stop monkeying about . . .

'Michelle, ma belle, Sunday monkey play no piano song, no piano song' is, of course, a mishearing of The Beatles' words, 'Michelle, ma belle, sont des mots qui vont très bien ensemble, très bien ensemble.'

'Rainy days and monkeys always get me down'

No, Karen and Richard Carpenter hadn't had an unfortunate encounter with some troublesome primates. In fact they were singing about 'Rainy Days and Mondays'.

Grey Days

'Grey Day Holidays'

A common mishearing of 'Grade-A holidays'

'You make me happy, because I'm great'

The correct lyric from 'You Are My Sunshine'
by Jimmy Davis and Charles Mitchell is 'You make
me happy, when skies are grey'

'Here comes the rain again
Falling on my head like a locomotion'

In 'Here Comes the Rain Again' by Eurythmics, it was a
'new emotion' that came falling down

'For the Lord God omnipotent, rain please'

From the Hallelujah Chorus in Handel's *Messiah* came the
line 'For the Lord God omnipotent reigneth'

'Don't reign in my parade'

'Don't rain on my parade' comes from the 1964 musical
Funny Girl

For Old Times' Sake

When I'm six and four

'Will you still need me, will you still feed me, when I'm sixty-four' is the correct version of The Beatles' lyric from 'When I'm Sixty-Four', but my two young children decided the song was clearly about their own ages: 'Will you still need me, will you still feed me, when I'm six and four.'

Before you meet your maker

Sometimes our frame of reference can colour our hearing. For example, a lady was on her way back from visiting a friend who was recovering from heart surgery. She decided to call in on her own daughter and granddaughter. Before leaving their home, she asked what she could get her granddaughter for a birthday present. 'A Shaker Maker, please!' the girl replied, enthusiastically. 'A pacemaker?' questioned Gran. 'Good heavens, what do you want with one of those at your age?'

Right, in someone's mind

A child visiting her grandfather in hospital listened to her mother in discussion with a consultant. Her grandfather was showing signs of senile dementia.

CHILD: 'Mummy, I know why Granddad forgets my name now.'
MOTHER: 'Darling, the doctor thinks he's got . . .'
CHILD: 'Old timers, I know. I heard the doctor say it.'

Home sweet home

Meanwhile, a fit and healthy grandmother was amused when one of her grandchildren asked her when she would be going to the 'tyrant home' like his other granny. 'I hope this was just a slip of the tongue and not his view of the retirement home,' she said.

The old of today

CHILD: 'Granny, are you deaf?'
GRANNY: 'No, I'm not dead yet, dear, just a bit deaf.'

It's the Way
You Tell Them

▬▬▬▬

SOMETIMES it is other people who make hard work for our ears. Try these spoonerisms for example:

She's still keeping up fainting paces

What you just said was a lack of pies

He pulled on his cat flap

That's a bad salad you just sang

Do you have a plaster man for the pleating and humming?

Please remove your junk of heap from my drive

It's a sale of two titties

I've applied for the job of Rental Deceptionist

How is that supposed to tease my ears?

It's roaring with pain, but I'll brave it with my umbrella

I've signed up to 'Wave the sails'!

You smell, you know. Go and shake a tower

Miscellaneous Mishearings

T HE FOLLOWING tales aren't strictly mondegreens, but they're general aural misunderstandings along with a couple of jokes, and far too funny to be omitted from this book.

What's in a name?

'They asked me to change my name. I suppose they were afraid that if my real name, Diana Fluck, was in lights, and one of the lights blew . . .'

In her autobiography, the legendary screen actress and sex symbol Diana Dors (1931–84) recalls the occasion she was asked to open a fête in her home town of Swindon. Before the event, Dors had lunch with the local vicar, during which she told him her real name. Arriving at the event, the clergyman duly announced the famous attendee:

'Ladies and gentlemen, it is with great pleasure that I introduce to you our star guest. We all love her, especially as she is our local girl. I therefore feel it right to introduce her by her real name; Ladies and gentlemen, please welcome the very lovely Miss Diana Clunt.'

It's just a scratch, honest

A conversation cancelling a planned meeting with a friend:

LADY: 'Look I won't be able to make it. You know I had my car returned the other day, well it had a nick in it and I'm waiting for the man to arrive to repair it. I think they nicked it as they got it off the lorry on to the drive.'

FRIEND, screaming to her husband: 'Danny, Jo's had her car stolen! They nicked it off the lorry as it was being driven on to her drive. . . . '

At this point, half amused and half concerned, the lady felt the need to put an end to the drama.

Flights of fancy

A biology teacher was trying to explain to her class about birds' feathers. 'The flight feathers are for flying,' she said. 'But can anyone tell me what down is?'

'The feathers that make the bird come down,' piped up one student.

> ### 'Demons are a ghoul's best friend'
>
> Or should that be 'Diamonds are a girl's best friend'?

Hither, page, and stand by me

A teacher was somewhat surprised when a mother complained to her about the part her son had been given in the school Christmas play. 'He doesn't want to be a piece of paper,' she said. The teacher was initially puzzled, but then saw the funny side of things. 'Your son is the *page*. I think he must have misunderstood.'

A case of miscasting

During a trip to the USA before the war, the British politician Sir Samuel Hoare visited Sam Goldwyn in his office at the MGM studios. After a pleasant chat, Hoare got up to go. Goldwyn bade him goodbye and then, as an afterthought, added, 'And my best to Lady W. . . .'

> *'Ghostwriters in the sky'*
>
> A mishearing of 'Ghost Riders In The Sky'
> by Johnny Cash

> **'A chance to find the fuel mix for the plane'**
>
> According to Duran Duran's 'A View to a Kill',
> one should be finding 'a phoenix for the flame'

MAN: 'Do you want to dance?'

WOMAN: 'No.'

MAN: 'Sorry, I think you misheard me . . . I said, "You look fat in those pants."'

You've been egg-corned

Contemplating my children's noses, I remarked to a friend that they would need blow jobs if their noses grew to be as long as mine and as wide as their father's.

I probably wouldn't have realized what I'd said if it hadn't been for the shocked expression on my friend's face as she tried to make sense of my slip of the tongue.

> **'Ain't No Woman Like a One-Eyed Goat'**
>
> A mondegreen of 'Ain't No Woman (Like the One I've Got)' by the Four Tops

> **'Beelzebub is a devil with his sights on me'**
>
> A mishearing of 'Beelzebub has a devil put aside for me' in Queen's 'Bohemian Rhapsody'

Soup of the day

A ninety-five-year-old widower receives a surprising gift when a prostitute arrives on his doorstep and tells him she's his birthday present.

'I'm here to give you super sex,' she says, to which the old man replies, 'I'll take the soup.'

> **'The ocean will be yours'**
>
> A mishearing of the song 'Emotionally Yours' by Bob Dylan

Final Words

'It's a rare person who wants to hear
what he doesn't want to hear.'

DICK CAVETT (1936–)

'When we hear news we should always wait
for the sacrament of confirmation.'

VOLTAIRE (1694–1778),
letter to le Comte d'Argental,
28 August 1760